Welcome to the Peace of Mind Community!

Stay Informed

Peace of Mind's website and monthly newsletter offer practices you can use in the classroom and updates about events, training and resources. Visit our website and join our mailing list to keep up to date.

Get Support

If you are new to us, consider taking our 2-hour online course "Getting Started with Peace of Mind." For the link, visit the "Educators" section on our website.

Prepare to Teach

Find the materials you need for this curriculum in the "Shop" section of our website.

TeachPeaceofMind.org

Questions? Comments?

We'd love to hear from you!

info@TeachPeaceofMind.org

Support for
Peace of Mind

*Peace [of Mind] Class with Ms. Diesner is something I personally look forward to
as a teacher. I have the privilege of witnessing my students begin their journey
of finding their center and their place of stillness. Even with very young children,
it is possible. I think Peace [of Mind] Class empowers these little ones to have a
way to recognize, channel, confront, and engage their emotions.*

Irene Taguian, Pre-Kindergarten and Special Education Teacher

*I have found that Peace [of Mind] Class, and mindfulness in particular, has been
especially helpful for students who struggle with controlling emotions and are
easily upset. We take time each day to practice, and then students are able to
practice on their own later as needed.*

Liz Ritchie, Kindergarten Teacher

*I find Peace [of Mind] Class helps the students get in touch with their feelings,
and teaches them how to cope with situations in and out of the classroom.
Implementing Mindful Moments during breaks helps students, and they are
able to focus better in class and complete their assignments in a timely matter.*

Lynda Henderson, Kindergarten Aide

*The hard work and dedication that Jillian puts into teaching Mindfulness at
Lafayette has paid off in major ways. Most notably is the fact that we no longer
have a place where children who misbehave are sent. The need no longer exists
because practicing Mindfulness has eliminated it.*

Jacqueline Snowden, Assistant Principal

*Mindfulness has taught our students how to focus and develop their sense
of self-awareness and concentration. Additionally, our students are kind
and cooperative but most importantly, inclusive, which is remarkable in our
changing society.*

Stephanie Mayhew, Assistant Principal

The *Peace of Mind*™ Program

Peace of Mind Core Curriculum for Early Childhood

Peace of Mind Core Curriculum for First and Second Grade

Peace of Mind Core Curriculum for Third to Fifth Grade

Peace of Mind Curriculum for Grades 4 and 5

TeachPeaceofMind.org

Peace of Mind Inc., Washington, D.C. 20015
TeachPeaceofMind.org
Copyright 2016 Jillian Diesner and Peace of Mind Inc.

Managing Editor: Cheryl Cole Dodwell
Cover and interior design: Schwa Design Group
Logo: Pittny Creative

ISBN 978-0-9976954-1-0
Library of Congress Control Number: 2016944555

Published 2017

Contents

Introduction   1

I. Curriculum Overview   3
    Curriculum At-A-Glance   3
    The Peace of Mind Program   6
    American School Counselor Alignment   9
    Teaching Strategies GOLD: Social Emotional Learning Objectives   11
    District of Columbia Early Learning Standards: Social Emotional   11
        Development
    Maryland Public Schools Standard   12

II. How to Use this Curriculum   13
    Lesson Planning   13
    Materials   14
    Required Books and Videos   14
    Optional Books and Videos   14
    A Note on Puppets   16

III. Peace of Mind for Early Childhood   19

IV. Curriculum Goals   20

Unit 1 – Mindful Bodies, Mindful Breaths   21

    Mindfulness Skills – Mindful Body Position & Belly Breathing   21
        Week 1: Introduction to Peace of Mind Class and Mindfulness   22
        Week 2: Mindful Breathing with Flowers   26
        Week 3: Animal Breaths   30
        Week 4: Using My Body to Listen   34
        Week 5: What is Focus?   39

Unit 2 – Mindful of My Feelings and Thoughts   45

    Mindfulness Skills – Noticing Emotions & Noticing Thoughts   45
        Week 6: New Friends and Kindness Pals   46
        Week 7: Noticing My Feelings   51
        Week 8: Feelings Can Be Different Sizes   57
        Week 9: Thoughts and Thought Bubbles   62
        Week 10: Others Have Thoughts and Feelings, Too   67

Unit 3 – Mindful of Others   71

    Mindfulness Skills – Heartfulness & Gratitude   71
        Week 11: Heartfulness and Kindness   72
        Week 12: We're All On the Same Team   76

Week 13: Sharing and Taking Turns 81

Week 14: Needs and Wants 85

Week 15: What is a Compliment? 89

Unit 4 – Mindful Senses and My Brain 93

Mindfulness Skills: Sensory Experiences of Hearing, Seeing, Touching, Smelling and Eating 93

Week 16: Mindful Hearing & Introduction to the Brain 94

Week 17: Mindful Seeing & The Hippocampus 101

Week 18: Mindful Touch & The Overprotective Amydgala 106

Week 19: Mindful Smell & More Overprotective Amygdala 111

Week 20: Mindful Taste & My Growing Brain 116

Unit 5 – Mindful Self-Calming 123

Mindfulness Skills: Body Scan & Muscle Relaxation 123

Week 21: Mindful or Mindless? 124

Week 22: Choosing Kind 129

Week 23: Calming My Body 135

Week 24: More Ways to Calm Down 141

Week 25: Games and Big Feelings 145

Unit 6 – Mindful Problem Solving 151

Mindfulness Skills: Visualization & Positive Self-Talk 151

Week 26: How Big is My Problem? 152

Week 27: What is a Conflict? 158

Week 28: My Toolbox 162

Week 29: More Tools for Conflicts 167

Week 30: Heroes 172

Closing Activities - Student Choice of Mindfulness Activity 179

Week 31: Peace Is… 180

Week 32: Peace in Me 184

Resources 187

Reproducible Materials for Lessons 189

Book, Videos and Card Decks 198

Resources for Teachers and Parents 200

Bibliography 201

Credits 204

Acknowledgements 201

About the Author 206

Introduction

This curriculum was developed over the course of many years through my work as an elementary school counselor at Lafayette Elementary School in Washington D.C. Like many school counselors, I started out using a simple character education program with my students. We spent time learning about honesty, respect, and other positive character traits. After a couple of years of this, I began to accept that these lessons were not changing my students' behavior, despite my best efforts. Then one day a student asked, "so when are we going to learn some new vocabulary words?" I realized we needed to dig deeper and go beyond the vocabulary-type lessons to really teach kids how to "do" these words on a more profound level.

Around this same time, my colleague Linda Ryden was developing and expanding her *Peace of Mind* program, an elementary school curriculum that integrates mindfulness, social and emotional learning and conflict resolution skills. Linda had been teaching *Peace of Mind* to students in upper grades at Lafayette for many years with great results. Our older students were learning how solve conflicts, even when they felt angry, to practice kindness, even with children who weren't their friends, and to empathize with others. We realized that the strength of the *Peace of Mind* curriculum was its foundation: mindfulness. All of the social and emotional skills were taught after students acquired and began to practice foundational mindfulness skills.

After seeing the impact of including mindfulness in the curriculum for older students, I realized this was the missing piece in our early childhood classrooms. We needed a *Peace of Mind* for our littlest learners. Working with Linda, and drawing on my own many years of experience working with 3 to 6 year olds, I developed this curriculum with my students over the next several years. Now they have tools, rather than just knowledge of vocabulary, to manage their bodies and emotions in a better way. The information they are learning feels deeper and more valuable, and they are able to tell me how they calm down with mindful breathing and work out conflicts using tools they've learned in class. They move on to the next elementary grades having a foundation of mindfulness that can continue to be built upon.

The *Peace of Mind Core Curriculum for Early Childhood* not only teaches mindfulness, empathy and foundational conflict resolution strategies, but also helps to guide the youngest students into the rhythms of school, and prepares them to learn how to focus their attention, build healthy relationships, and become peacemakers.

We hope that the lessons here help you in building more positive and inclusive classrooms and schools. Thank you for taking up this important work!

Jillian

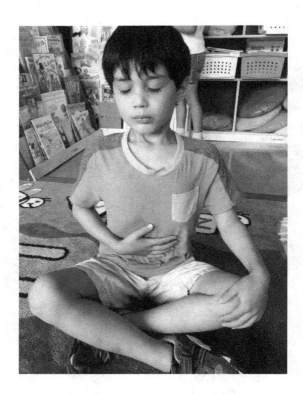

Curriculum Overview

Peace of Mind for Pre-Kindergarten and Kindergarten Curriculum At-A-Glance

Unit 1 - Mindful Bodies, Mindful Breaths						
Week	**Mindfulness Skill**	**Target Quiet Time**	**Lesson Objective(s)**	**ASCA Standards**	**Materials**	**Kindness Pals**
1. Intro to Class	Mindful bodies vs. regular bodies	20 seconds	Compare Mindful bodies to regular bodies; demonstrate procedures and routines for class; describe "peace"	B-SMS 1	Bell, puppet	Not introduced
2. Mindful Breathing with Flowers	Mindful bodies vs. regular bodies; belly breathing		Model and practice deep breathing	B-SMS 2	Bell, flower picture	
3. Animal Breaths	Belly breathing		Bring attention to breaths, contrast shallow breaths and deep breaths	B-SMS 2	Bell, puppet	
4. Using My Body to Listen	Belly breathing		Bring awareness to various body parts that help us pay attention effectively	B-SMS 2	Bell	
5. What is Focus?	Belly breathing		Apply previously-learned listening skills to practice following instructions and maintaining focus during a group game	B-SMS 1 B-SMS 4	Bell, 1 small item for each student	

Unit 2 - Mindful of My Feelings and Thoughts						
6. New Friends & Kindness Pals	Attending to feelings	30 seconds	Demonstrate purpose and routines of kindness pals; practice basic communication skills	B-SS 1 B-SS 2	Bell, Kindness Pal list	New pals; procedures and routines
7. Noticing My Feelings	Attending to feelings		Attend to feelings; identify, define, and act out at least 5 feelings words	B-SS 1 B-SS 2	Bell, puppet	Tell a feeling
8. Feelings Can Be Different Sizes	Attending to feelings		Identify feelings sizes using a 1-5 scale; define "calming down;" use deep breathing to calm down	B-SMS 1 B-LS 4	Bell, puppet, thermometer	Tell about a big feeling and calming down
9. My Thoughts and Thought Bubbles	Attending to thoughts		Explore thoughts and thought bubbles; use a thought bubble illustration to show something one is thinking about	B-LS 2 B-SS 2	Bell, 1 thought bubble template per student; new KP list	New pals; share your thought bubble picture
10. Others Have Thoughts and Feelings, Too	Attending to thoughts		Review concept of thought bubbles and apply to the thoughts and related feelings of others	B-SS 4	Bell, thought bubble picture	Name what your partner is thinking and feeling

Unit 3 - Mindful of Others

Week	Mindfulness Skill	Target Quiet Time	Lesson Objective(s)	ASCA Standards	Materials	Kindness Pals
11. Heartfulness and Kindness	Heartfulness		Practice sending good thoughts to others; define respect as being different and getting along	B-SS 4	Bell	Notice differences
12. We're on the Same Team	Heartfulness	40 sec.	Identify "teamwork" as working together to achieve something you can't do on your own; name the team they all belong to (the class)	B-SS 2 B-SS 7	Bell, floor puzzle new KP list	New pal greetings; tell about teams
13. Sharing and Taking Turns	Heartfulness		Practice sending good thoughts to oneself; define and practice sharing and taking turns	B-SS 6 B-SS 7	Bell, small items for sharing	Practice sharing and taking turns
14. Needs and Wants	Gratitude		Practice gratitude; contrast needs and wants	B-SS 3 B-SS 9	Bell	Tell three needs and give thanks
15. What is a compliment	Gratitude		Choose a person for whom one feels grateful; practice giving a compliment; notice how receiving a compliment feels	B-SS 2 B-SS 3	Bell, puppet; new KP list	New pals; give compliments to each other

Unit 4 – Mindful Senses and My Brain

Week	Mindfulness Skill	Target Quiet Time	Lesson Objective(s)	ASCA Standards	Materials	Kindness Pals
16. Mindful Hearing & Intro to Brain	Deepening sense of hearing		Applying mindfulness skills to hearing sounds; identify 3 parts of the brain	B-SS 1 B-LS 1	Bell, Brainy puppet; items that make sound	Model the three parts of the brain
17. Mindful Seeing & the Hippocampus	Deepening sense of sight		Apply mindfulness skills to seeing; explore role of hippocampus in memory	B-SMS 2 B-LS 1	Bell, Brainy puppet	Use your hippocampus to tell a memory
18. Mindful Touch & the Overprotective Amygdala	Deepening sense of touch	50 sec.	Apply mindfulness skills to the sense of touch; explore roles of hippocampus, amygdala and PFC in reactions to sensations	B-SMS 2 B-SMS 7 B-SS 2	Bell, Brainy puppet, new KP list	New pals; name comfortable and uncomfortable items touched
19. Mindful Smell & More Overprotective Amygdala	Deepening sense of smell		Apply mindfulness skills to the sense of smell; explore roles of amygdala, hippocampus and PFC in reactions to smells	B-SMS 7 B-LS 1	Bell, Brainy puppet, various items to smell	Tell favorite and least favorite smells
20. Mindful Taste & My Growing Brain	Deepening sense of taste; using all five senses during eating		Apply mindfulness skills to the sense of taste and eating; explore roles of the amygdala, hippocampus and PFC in taste.	B-SMS 7 B-LS 1	Bell, Brainy puppet, raisin/ snack for class	Tell favorite and least favorite foods; name a food to try again

Unit 5 - Mindful Self-Calming

Week	Mindfulness Skill	Target Quiet Time	Lesson Objective(s)	ASCA Standards	Materials	Kindness Pals
21. Mindful or Mindless?	Body scan	60 sec.	Scan bodies to notice feelings; synthesize previous lessons on using our brains to define actions as "mindful" or "mindless"	B-LS 1 B-SS 2 B-SS 5	Bell; new KP list	New pals; tell about doing something mindfully and mindlessly

Week	Mindfulness Skill	Target Quiet Time	Lesson Objective(s)	ASCA Standards	Materials	Kindness Pals
Unit 5 - Mindful Self-Calming *Continued*						
22. Choosing Kind	Body Scan		Relate "making a choice" to intentional actions, and practice using intention to make mindful and kind choices with others	B-SS 4 B-SS 9	Bell, puppets	Tell about a kind choice
23. Calming my Body	Body Scan		Use Body Scanning to notice feelings; identify and practice a strategy for calming down	B-SMS 7 B-SMS 10	Bell, thermometer, Brainy puppet	Practice body scan and breaths for calming down
24. More Ways to Calm Down	Muscle relaxation	60 sec.	Review and practice strategies for self-calming; name and practice at least three strategies for calming oneself	B-SMS 7 B-SMS 10 B-SS 2	Bell, one Calm Down page per student, new KP list	New pals; share and evaluate strategies with pals
25. Games and Big Feelings	Muscle relaxation		Apply learned concept of "mindful actions" to choosing, playing, and winning or losing games.	B-SMS 7 B-SMS 10 B-SS 9	Bell, puppets	Play "Rock, Paper, Scissors" to model staying calm during games
Unit 6 – Mindful Problem-Solving						
26. How Big is My Problem?	Visualization		Use senses to visualize being in a calming place; categorize problems as small, medium or large	B-LS 1 B-SMS 7	Bell, ther-mometer	Tell about a big problem and if your reaction matched
27. What is Conflict?	Visualization		Use visualization as a strategy for self-calming; identify conflicts as small problems between two or more people	B-SS 2 B-SS 6	Bell, puppets, new KP list	New pals; Tell about a conflict it's size
28. My Toolbox	Visualization	60+ sec.	Use visualization as a method of self-calming; define and apply concept of using tools as a way to solve conflicts.	B-SS 6 B-SS 2	Bell, puppets,	Practice using the tools with a pal
29. More Tools for Conflicts	Positive self-talk		Use positive self-talk as a method of self-calming; define and apply three conflict resolution strategies to address common problems children may have in school	B-SMS 7	Bell, puppets	Practice using the tools with a pal
30. Heroes	Positive self-talk		Practice positive self-talk as a method of self-calming; demonstrate advocat-ing for others who are being teased or picked-on.	B-SS 8 B-SS 2	Bell, new KP list	New pals/final; practice speaking up for a pal teased
Closing Activities						
31. Peace Is…	Student Choice	60+ sec.	Synthesize concepts learned through-out the year to form a sensory-based definition of peace.	B-LS 2 B-SS 1	Bell, one Peace Is… booklet for each student	Teacher Choice
32. Peace In Me	Student Choice		Evaluate self-calming concepts learned throughout the year to select those that are most helpful	B-LS 1 B-SMS 7	Bell, one Peace In Me page for each student	Teacher Choice

The Peace of Mind Program

The Peace of Mind Program includes innovative curricula for elementary school students that integrate mindfulness practice, social and emotional learning, and conflict resolution. The goal of the **Peace of Mind Program** is to help shift school cultures toward kindness and inclusion.

Peace of Mind for Early Childhood students is the very first step on what we hope is a long and positive journey on the path of mindfulness and social and emotional maturity. Like the other curricula in the **Peace of Mind** series, this beginning curriculum includes three critical and interwoven components:

 Mindfulness

 Social and Emotional Learning

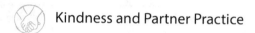 Kindness and Partner Practice

Mindfulness

Every lesson begins with mindfulness practice. Since this is most students' first introduction to mindfulness, the concepts are taught slowly, gently, and with much repetition. The mindfulness sessions are intentionally short initially, and gradually grow to a minute or more by the end of the curriculum. Given the relatively short duration of each session, mindfulness practice for Early Childhood students is referred to as a **Mindful Moment.**

The mindfulness sessions for Early Childhood are more adult-directed than those in the *Peace of Mind* curricula for older grades due to the developmental needs of young children, who may find it difficult to sit still and quietly for very long without hearing any instructions.

The mindfulness skills taught in this curriculum are designed to build from week to week, moving from simple deep breathing to cognitive regulation strategies. Here is a sequential list of the mindfulness skills that are taught in this curriculum:

1. Mindful body position
2. Deep belly breathing
3. Awareness of emotions
4. Awareness of thoughts
5. Heartfulness
6. Gratitude
7. Sensory experiences (mindful listening, smelling, seeing, eating)
8. Body scanning
9. Muscle relaxation
10. Visualization
11. Positive self-talk

 Social and Emotional Learning

Every lesson contains a **Social and Emotional Learning (SEL)** component. These lessons involve puppets, stories, games, and occasional optional videos to illustrate the skills taught. The SEL components of each lesson are grouped into six units that follow the rhythm of a traditional school year and the inter-personal development of very young children. Each lesson is also interwoven with the mindfulness skills listed above, and each mindfulness skill helps rein-force the SEL topic.

Here is a sequential list of the unit topics:

1. Mindful Bodies, Mindful Breaths
2. Mindful of My Feelings and Thoughts
3. Mindful of Others
4. Mindful Senses and My Brain
5. Mindful Self-Calming
6. Mindful Problem Solving
7. Closing Activities/Curriculum Review

Kindness Pals

The final component of each lesson in this curriculum, starting in the second unit, is **Kindness and Partner Practice**, also simply known as "Kindness Pals." Because children are still adjusting to being in school and figuring out how to "be" in school, we don't introduce Kindness Pals until Unit 2 (Week 6) when students are a bit more settled and able to think beyond themselves in the classroom.

Kindness Pals is a very engaging activity that achieves several goals:

- To remind the children to make kindness part of their daily lives. Doing kind things for their Kindness Pals spills over into their treatment of others.

- To develop the habit of treating people with kindness through regular practice.

- To give children opportunities to get to know each other and to "find the good" in others whom they might not have gotten along with in the past or whom they think they just don't like.

Once we introduce Kindness Pals, students will keep their same pals for several weeks before changing to a new pal. In this curriculum there is a prompt to change pals every three weeks. Changing pals when the month changes can be helpful in terms of planning, and this ensures multiple partner changes over the course of the year. Feel free to use a different schedule that works for your pacing.

It is recommended, however, that pals stay the same for two or more weeks in Pre-K and Kindergarten. They will not always remember their pals after just one turn working with that person during *Peace of Mind* class, and will not usually be able to work independently with their Kindness Pals between weekly *Peace of Mind* classes. Classroom teachers may use the Kindness Pal partners for other partnering activities within the class routines.

It is equally important to allow the children to get a chance to work with many of the other children in the class. Changing pals often enough to allow many different partners gives students practice in building relationships with diverse classmates.

Every lesson in Unit 2, after Kindness Pals are introduced, will give detailed instructions and scripts for the instructor to follow. The scripts are provided throughout Unit 2 to give you time to make this a comfortable and predictable component of each *Peace of Mind* class. In Units 3-6, the Kindness Pal section will simply give a numbered list of actions students can take together during this portion of the class. If you need a refresher on the Kindness Pal script as you are teaching Units 3-6, just flip back to Unit 2.

Peace of Mind for Pre-Kindergarten and Kindergarten uses **gender neutral language** to reflect the inclusive practices being taught and meet the needs of our diverse children. Instead of "boys and girls" you might say "lovely learners," "fabulous friends," or "awesome amigos" in these scripts.

The **Opening** and **Closing** of each *Peace of Mind* lesson are brief, but important, anchors at the beginning and end of class that also serve to link the lessons and encourage students to practice the skills learned in class throughout the week.

Optional Lesson Extensions are included at the end of each lesson, and can be used to extend the time spent on the original lesson or to supplement between lessons throughout the week.

American School Counselor Association Alignment

The primary goals of *Peace of Mind for Early Childhood* are to help students establish basic foundational mindfulness skills; to learn to work in groups; to learn basic self-regulation and problem-solving skills; and to nurture the innate kindness and acceptance in each child. In the process of teaching these skills, *Peace of Mind* fulfills many of the ASCA goals for young children.

Peace of Mind for Early Childhood is aligned with ASCA Mindsets & Behaviors for Student Success, and the majority of the Category 2 Behavior Standards are met through this curriculum. The *Peace of Mind* Curriculum Series also supports the majority of the six important Category 1 Mindset Standards for all students:

Mindset 1: Belief in development of whole self, including a healthy balance of mental, social-emotional, and physical well-being

Mindset 2: Self-confidence in the ability to succeed

Mindset 3: Sense of belonging in the school environment

Mindset 6: Positive attitude toward work and learning

Specific ASCA Behavior Standards covered by this curriculum include the following:

Learning Strategy 1: Demonstrate critical thinking skills to make informed decisions

Learning Strategy 2: Demonstrate creativity

Learning Strategy 4: Apply self-motivation and self-direction to learning

Learning Strategy 9: Gather evidence and consider multiple perspectives to make informed decisions

Self-Management Skills 1: Demonstrate ability to assume responsibility

Self-Management Skills 2: Demonstrate self-discipline and self-control

Self-Management Skills 4: Demonstrate ability to delay immediate gratification for long-term rewards

Self-Management Skills 5: Demonstrate perseverance to achieve long and short-term goals

Self-Management Skills 6: Demonstrate ability to overcome barriers to learning

Self-Management Skills 7: Demonstrate effective coping skills when faced with a problem

Self-Management Skills 9: Demonstrate personal safety skills

Self-Management Skills 10: Demonstrate ability to manage transitions and ability to adapt to changing situations and responsibilities

Social Skills 1: Use effective oral and written communication skills and listening skills

Social Skills 2: Create positive and supportive relationships with other students

Social Skills 3: Create relationships with adults that support success

Social Skills 4: Demonstrate empathy

Social Skills 5: Demonstrate ethical decision-making and social responsibility

Social Skills 6: Use effective collaboration and cooperation skills

Social Skills 7: Use leadership and teamwork skills to work effectively in diverse teams

Social Skills 8: Demonstrate advocacy skills and ability to assert self when necessary

Social Skills 9: Demonstrate social maturity and behaviors appropriate to the situation and environment

Teaching Strategies GOLD: Social Emotional Learning Objectives

Peace of Mind for Early Childhood is also aligned to meet social-emotional learning objectives in the Teaching Strategies GOLD assessment. These include:

1. Regulates own emotions and behaviors
   a. Manages feelings
   b. Follows limits and expectations
   c. Takes care of own needs appropriately

2. Establishes and sustains positive relationships
   a. Forms relationships with adults
   b. Responds to emotional cues
   c. Interacts with peers
   d. Makes friends

3. Participates cooperatively and constructively in group situations
   a. Balances needs and rights of self and others
   b. Solves social problems

District of Columbia Early Learning Standards: Social Emotional Development

Peace of Mind for Early Childhood is also aligned to meet the six social-emotional early learning standards the District of Columbia has adopted from the Common Core State Standards. These include:

Standard	Description
26.	Expresses a variety of feelings and learns to manage them
27.	Recognizes the feelings and rights of others, and responds appropriately
28.	Manages own behavior
29.	Develops positive relationships with adults
30.	Engages and plays with peers
31.	Resolves conflict with others

Maryland Public Schools Standard

Peace of Mind for Early Childhood is also aligned to meet the Maryland Public Schools Standard for Mental and Emotional Health for Kindergarten.

Standard 1: Students will demonstrate the ability to use mental and emotional health knowledge, skills, and strategies to enhance one's self concept and one's relationship with others.

Peace of Mind related performance Indicators for this standard include:

A. Communication

    1.K.A.1. Recognize Methods of Communication:

        1.K.A.1a. Demonstrate positive communication among peers.

B. Emotions

    1.K.B.1 Examine emotions and responses to various situations

        1.K.B.1.a Identify basic emotions/feelings.

        1.K.B.1.b Demonstrate expressions of basic emotions/feelings

E. Character Traits

    1.K.E.1 b. Identify actions to make a friend.

How to Use
This Curriculum

Peace of Mind is different from other SEL programs in that mindfulness serves as the foundation for all of the social and emotional lessons in the curriculum. Mindfulness increases children's attention and focus, enhancing lessons for students and teacher alike. Based on over a decade of experience teaching **Peace of Mind**, we believe that SEL lessons following mindfulness practice are experienced more deeply and fully by the students.

Peace of Mind is designed to be used by classroom teachers as part of the weekly classroom routine, or by counselors or specials teachers who visit class-rooms on a weekly basis.

This curriculum is comprised of 32 sequential weekly lessons. All of the lessons begin with mindfulness practice. After foundational mindfulness skills have been established and reviewed, the lessons build to include practice in listening and focusing, recognizing thoughts and feelings, respecting and working with others, using simplified brain science to make kind choices, and self-calming.

The lessons are designed to be taught sequentially within the Unit, as each lesson builds upon the skills previously learned. All of the mindfulness practices benefit from repetition throughout the week if possible.

Lesson Planning:

Each class in this curriculum is designed to take about 30 minutes. Given that the attention span of young children is much shorter than this, each lesson is broken down into three consistent parts, each lasting about 10 minutes. Providing a small movement break between the parts may be needed initially. After Unit 1, the class will always end with Kindness Pals, a segment that incor-porates movement and talking.

Part 1 - Introduction and Mindful Moment

Part 2 – SEL Lesson

Part 3 - Kindness Pals and Closing

Sticking to this format will help keep little bodies engaged and attentive. Occasionally the lesson will also involve moving to seats to draw, which provides movement as well.

Materials:

- Bell or chime - Choose a bell or chime with a full, clear sound that continues for many seconds after ringing it.
- Two puppets - One of your choosing and Peace of Mind's **Brainy the Puppet™**
- Kindness Pal lists – Included in the Appendix
- **Week 5**: Small tangible items such as a rock, marble, or paper clip for each student to hold during the game *Don't Lose Your Focus!*
- **Week 12**: Floor Puzzle with enough pieces for each student to have one. For most classes a 2x3 floor puzzle with 24 pieces will be sufficient.
- **Week 13**: Stuffed animal or other object that can be passed around in a circle, and enough small toys or other interesting items for partners to share.
- **Week 19**: Several different strong-smelling items to pass around for students to sniff.
- **Week 20**: One raisin for each student to taste.

Books and Videos

There are no required books and videos for this curriculum. However, we suggest the following optional materials that you might use to extend your lessons.

Optional Books and Videos

Week	Book or Card Deck	Video
1	*The Peace Book* by Todd Parr	
2	*Take A Deep Breath* by Sue Graves	*Belly Breathe* by Sesame Street

Week	Book or Card Deck	Video
3	*Yoga Pretzels: 50 Fun Yoga Activities for Kids and Grownups* Card Deck by Leah Kalish and Tara Gruber	
4	*Whole Body Listening Larry at School* by Elizabeth Sautter and Kristen Wilson	*The Biscotti Kid* by Sesame Street
5		*Cookies of the Caribbean* by Sesame Street
6	*Have You Filled A Bucket Today?* By Carol McCloud	
7	*Glad Monster, Sad Monster* by Ed Emberly and Anne Miranda *Today I Feel Silly* by Jamie Lee Curtis *My Many-Colored Days* by Dr. Suess Todd Parr's Feelings Flashcards	
8	*When My Worries Get Too Big* by Kari Dunn Buron	*Belly Breathe* by Sesame Street
9	*What is A Thought? (A Thought is A Lot!)* by Amy Kahofer and Jack Pransky	
11	*The Sneetches* by Dr. Seuss *It's Okay to be Different* by Todd Parr	
12	*Swimmy* by Leo Lionni *Everyone Matters* by Pat Thomas	
13	*Should I Share My Ice Cream?* by Mo Willems *Share and Take Turns* by Cheri J. Meiners	
14	*The Thankful Book* by Todd Parr	
17	*The Fantastic, Elastic Brain* by JoAnn M. Deak	
20	*I Will Never Not Ever Eat a Tomato* by Lauren Child	
21	*Furry Potter* by Sesame Street	
22		*Fill Your Bucket* by The Learning Station

Week	Book or Card Deck	Video
23	*Waiting Is Not Easy!* by Mo Willems	*Star S'mores* by Sesame Street
25	*Howard B. Wigglebottam Learns About Sportsmanship: Winning Isn't Everything* by Howard Binkow; *Sally the Sore Loser: A Story About Winning and Losing* by Frank J. Sileo	
27	*"The Zax"* in *The Sneetches & Other Stories* by Dr. Seuss	*"Word of the Day is Conflict"* by Sesame Street
28	*The Day No One Played Together: A Story About Compromise* by Donalisa Helsley	
29	*The Berenstain Bears and the Trouble With Friends* by Stan Berenstain *The Recess Queen* by Alexis O'neill and Laura Huliska-Beith *A Children's Book About Teasing* by Joy Berry	
31	*What Does Peace Feel Like?* By Vladimir Radunsky	

A Note On Puppets

Puppet Logistics

Using the puppets may feel challenging initially. To help you, specific scripts are provided for the first two units of the curriculum, and again in the first lessons of Unit 4 when the new puppet, Brainy, is introduced. It is perfectly fine to read directly from the scripts included here while you use the puppet with a class. Remember, all eyes will be on the puppet and not on your face. Just keep the hand moving as you read and most children won't even notice!

In most other lessons beginning with Unit 3, specific scripts for the puppets are replaced with general guidelines so that you may create your own dialogue with the puppets.

Go ahead, be creative and try to lose any self-consciousness! The laughter and delight of the children will let you know this is an important and engaging component of **Peace of Mind** class for Early Childhood students. They will also beg you week after week to bring the puppets back.

Puppet Benefits

There are many benefits to using puppets in your classroom:

Reviewing Information - You will find that if you repeat to the puppet whatever you just told the class, it gives you a great way to review the material you have taught and allows the children to feel as if they know something the puppet does not.

Children as the Leaders – The puppet can make "mistakes" that children often make, and then the children can point them out and tell the puppet what the mistakes were. This is a great way to de-personalize behaviors and talk about them in an objective way. It also allows children to laugh at themselves (the puppet) in a unique and enlightening way, and to be "experts" who teach the puppet new things.

Classroom Management - Bring out the puppet <u>only</u> when the class is quiet. Explain that if the children are talking too much the puppet won't be able to talk, and put it away. You can also say the puppet is shy and too much noise is frightening. The children will love the puppets so much, and get so excited when they come out, that this an important routine to establish. Don't be afraid to put the puppet away completely and not bring it out for the rest of the lesson if a class repeatedly is too rowdy. This will help make your next session smoother.

"The Talk" – At some point, you will find a student looking at you suspiciously and then shouting out, "Hey, that's just your *hand* and *you're* the one talking!" This realization might take longer than you would think, which just shows how the line between real and imaginary is so wonderfully subtle at this young age. When this happens, pause your story. Move the puppet to the side or behind your back, as if you don't want it to hear what you have to say. Tell the class you are going to let them in on a little secret, if they can agree to keep the secret. Kids love secrets, and they will vigorously agree. Then whisper loudly "The puppet isn't real! It IS just my hand and my voice making it talk. But isn't it more fun to hear the puppet tell you funny stories and act silly than it would be if it were just me up here talking to you? So can we all agree to keep this important secret so we can keep having fun with the puppet? Okay, great!" Then continue on with the lesson.

Choosing and using your own Puppet

Take some time to find a puppet that you will enjoy using. It's important to choose a puppet that has a good working mouth that opens and closes. (Many puppets' mouths do not.) I use a puppy dog named Paco, as I find it symbolic of the children at this young age: excitable, enthusiastic, and often very active. While I also incorporate a few different puppets with consistent personalities -- a shy, anxious lamb, a grouchy ladybug, and so on -- I have primarily stuck with Paco as the main puppet we use each week, and will refer to "Paco" in these scripts. Of course feel free to use whatever name you choose for your main puppet, and to incorporate other puppets as you feel comfortable doing so.

Using *Brainy the Puppet*™

Brainy the Puppet™ ("Brainy"), is introduced in Unit 4 to help you teach a simple version of brain science that supports lessons on calming and managing big feelings. Units 5 and 6 also contain several lessons with Brainy. Using a hand model of the brain developed by Dr. Daniel Siegel, this puppet teaches small children about three important parts of their brain:

- **Amygdala** – the thumb part of the puppet, kept tucked inside your fist until Amygdala speaks in the lessons.
- **Hippocampus** – the pickle-shaped area on the palm behind the Amygdala.
- **Pre-Frontal Cortex (PFC)** – the zig-zag area above Brainy's eyes.

Using *Brainy* as indicated in the lessons will help students recall the names and functions of these three important areas that work together to regulate emotions.

Puppet Alternatives

If using the puppets just doesn't work for you, instead use the scripts to tell the children stories about an imaginary friend/pet/relative/and so on. Use the Brainy puppet as a model for the brain, and tell the rest of the stories in the same manner as the Paco scripts.

Peace of Mind for Early Childhood

The **Peace of Mind Core Curriculum for Early Childhood** not only teaches mindfulness, empathy and foundational conflict resolution strategies, but also helps to guide the youngest students into the rhythms of school.

Here are a few strategies to help your lessons run smoothly for you and your students.

Circle and grouped seating If you start **Peace of Mind** early in the year, classroom procedures and routines may not be established yet. For instance, if a routine for carpet time/circle time has not yet been established, let children remain in their seats for these first few lessons. You may need to remind children that you can only hear one student speak at a time, so they must raise their hands quietly and wait to be called on before speaking out. Work with your class or the teacher of the class to develop routines for sitting in a circle, sitting in a group to listen to a story, moving back to seats, and so on. Some classes I've worked in use catchy names for these positions: frying pan (circle) and melting pot (grouped).

Quiet signal If you are teaching **Peace of Mind** to your own students, use the quiet signal you have already established during **Peace of Mind** time. If you are a teacher or counselor who goes into classrooms that are not your own to teach **Peace of Mind**, you will notice that each classroom has different quiet signals. If this is your situation, establish your own signal rather than trying to use the many different call-and-response signals used. A simple egg shaker, or similar soft sound that is different than the chime you will use for your Mindful Moments, works well. It is helpful to practice this explicitly every so often, especially after noticing that the children don't quiet down immediately upon hearing the signal.

Materials bag Choose a closed bag or container to bring class materials each week so that contents are not visible and can be kept out of sight. The materials listed above - bell or chime and puppets - will be the primary teaching tools for every **Peace of Mind** class. You may choose to add in books or other optional activities. Students will be highly curious about which materials you will be using (particularly whether or not there is a puppet) and it's helpful to use that suspense to your advantage in maintaining classroom management and routines.

Goals for Early Childhood Students

The goals of **Peace of Mind for Early Childhood** are simple but profound. Students will begin to:

- Establish basic foundational mindfulness skills that can develop into a life-long practice.

- Practice skills that support positive social and emotional growth, including working in groups, self-regulation, and resolving conflicts.

- Model and expand kindness and acceptance to help create a kinder and more inclusive culture in each classroom and school.

Unit 1
Mindful Bodies, Mindful Breaths

Mindfulness Skills – Mindful Body Position and Belly Breathing

Target quiet time during mindfulness ≅ 20 seconds

Week 1:
Introduction to *Peace of Mind* Class and Mindfulness

OBJECTIVES: Compare mindful bodies with regular bodies; demonstrate routines and procedures for Peace of Mind class; describe the word "peace."

> ASCA Standard:

B-SMS 1.
Demonstrate ability to assume responsibility

PREPARE: Bell or chime, hand puppet. You may substitute the name of your puppet for "Paco" in this lesson and those that follow.

Opening: *Hello and welcome to our very first **Peace of Mind** class! This year we are going to be learning all about peace and something called mindfulness. Each week when we have **Peace of Mind** class, we will always begin our class by practicing mindfulness.*

 Mindfulness Practice

Say: *Mindfulness sounds like "mind" and "full," and indeed our minds (**point to your head**) are usually full of all sorts of thoughts. When we practice mindfulness, we will try to make our minds full of what is happening right at this moment.*

*When we practice mindfulness, we sit up with straight backs (**model straightening upright**), get our bodies as still as possible, and become very quiet so we can <u>notice</u> all that is happening now. This is called our <u>mindful body</u>. Now, let's go back to our regular body (**shoulders slump, fidget, whisper, and so on**).*

Have the children practice moving between these two positions several times, then ask them to name some of the differences between the two positions.

Ask: *Which position, mindful bodies or regular bodies, will help us notice every little thing happening right now? Of course, our mindful bodies position! For that reason we will always get into our mindful bodies position to have our Mindful Moment. We will do this at the beginning of every **Peace of Mind** class when I say "Let's get in our mindful bodies."*

For now, you can stay in your regular body position while I show you two more things about our Mindful Moment.

Bring out your bell or chime. Ideally it will be a bell with a full, clear sound that continues for many seconds after ringing it.

Say: *After we get in our mindful bodies and spend a few moments noticing, I will ring this bell. Now, how long do you think my bell will ring? 1 second? 5 seconds? 25 seconds? Let's listen right now and see.*

Ring the bell loudly and then use your fingers to count silently how many seconds pass until the sound is gone. Point out that the bell doesn't just "ding" and stop after one second. If you listen carefully, the "ding" goes on and on, getting softer and softer until it stops after several seconds.

Say: *Every time we have a Mindful Moment, I'll ring a bell at the end. When I ring the bell, we will listen to the sound it makes until we don't hear it anymore. Then we will raise one hand to show we don't hear it. Let's try that right now.*

Practice. Spend a few minutes ringing the bell and modeling listening by pointing to your ear, raising your hand when it can no longer be heard. Some children will initially want to raise their hand immediately upon hearing the bell, but after a few times practicing, will get the hang of waiting and raising their hand when the sound stops.

Say: *Okay, now that we understand what to do, let's have our first official Mindful Moment. Let's all get in our mindful bodies, close or cover our eyes, and notice what's happening right now. You may notice sounds inside the classroom, your breathing, or something else. We will tell what we noticed in a few moments after I ring the bell and we raise our hand. For now, we will continue to be quiet and just notice all that is happening right now….*

After a period of quiet, ring the bell, raise your hand when it stops, and open your eyes. If you prefer to keep your eyes open to watch the class that is fine, too. Just be prepared to explain to the first student who points out that you are not closing your eyes that you, as the leader, might keep your eyes open to make sure everyone is okay.

Ask: *Who would like to share what they noticed?*

Call on all students who raise their hands, and encourage with specific statements such as "yes, your heartbeat is a very important thing to notice!"

> TEACHING TIP: Remind students that in order to all be heard when we're in a big group at school, the signal for wanting to say something is a quiet hand raise; that is, raising hands without calling out or otherwise

making noise. Because this is a skill that many are likely just beginning to develop this early in the year, you may want to take a moment here to model raising a hand to say something. You might want to take a few minutes here to practice quiet hand raises vs. noisy hand raises.

 Lesson

Say: *This is our very first **Peace of Mind** class, so today we are going to talk about the word <u>peace</u> and what it means. I brought a special puppet friend to help me. His name is Paco, and he's a little shy to meet you all, so you must get very quiet so you don't scare him.*

Once everyone is quiet, slowly bring out Paco and tell him you have a bunch of new friends for him to meet.

Say: *Paco, meet our class!*

Puppet: *Oh wow, hello kids, nice to meet you!*

Say: *Paco, this is our very first **Peace of Mind** class, so we are talking about what the word Peace means.*

Puppet: *Huh? Pizza? Well that's something that you eat, maybe with pepperoni on top.*

Say: *No, Paco, not pizza! Peace. Like "Peace and quiet."*

Puppet: *Ohhh, like a piece of pizza? I love pizza, ha-ha!*

Say: *No, Paco, the word "piece" like a piece of pizza sounds exactly like the word we're talking about, but it's spelled differently and has a different meaning. Let's see if the students can help you out. Who thinks they know what peace means?*

Call on several children to share what they think peace means. Then explain that it means <u>very calm and without any fighting or arguing</u>.

Puppet: *Ohhh, that kind of peace. Well, I feel peaceful when I eat a piece of pizza! I'm calm and not arguing, in fact I feel great!*

Say: *Yes, Paco, things that we love usually make us feel calm and peaceful. So for you, that might be pizza. In our weekly **Peace of Mind** class we will be learning how to keep our bodies calm and peaceful, and this will also keep our class a peaceful* *place, too.* **Puppet:** *Thanks for helping me learn what peace means. I hope I'll see you again soon, goodbye!*

Put Paco away out of sight and move to the final sharing activity.

Say: *Now we are going to each go around and say something that reminds us of peace. It could be a person, place, or thing you love. For Paco, it was pizza. Things and people we love usually make us feel very happy and peaceful, so let's see if you can name one. If not, we can pass you. I'll start by saying "my family."*

Moving in a circle or another clear order around the room, encourage each child to name something. If a students can't think of something or don't want to share yet, allow them to pass.

> TEACHING TIP: If you are a teacher or counselor going into classrooms that are not your own, you will notice that each class may have a different quiet signal/phrase. If this is the case, it is helpful to create your own signal and teach it to the students early on. For example, a simple maraca or egg shaker is great. To practice using this signal have the children say "talk talk talk" and then stop when you shake the shaker. Do this a few times until everyone immediately gets quiet at the sound of the shaker. Practice it now and again throughout the year.

 Kindness Pals: Not introduced until Unit 2

Closing: *Try to notice times when you feel peace in your body, and we'll talk about it in our next **Peace of Mind** class. Have a peace-filled week!*

Optional Lesson Extension:

Book: *The Peace Book* by Todd Parr. After children have named something that makes them feel peaceful, explain that this book shows some of the things the author thinks are peaceful. Read the story together, stopping to talk about some of the pictures and whether or not they make the students feel peaceful.

Class Poster: Use large poster paper for children to illustrate something that makes them feel peaceful. Label this "Peace Poster" and hang it in an area of the classroom where children can easily see it throughout the day.

Week 2
Mindful Breathing with Flowers

OBJECTIVE: Model and practice deep breathing.

PREPARE: Bell or chime, flower pictures (see Appendix) or an artificial flower

> ASCA Standard:

B-SMS 2.
Demonstrate
self-discipline and
self-control

Opening: *Hello again lovely learners! Did anyone feel peace in your body since I saw you last? If you did, I'd love to hear about it.*

Call on students who want to share, reminding students that peace is a feeling of calmness both inside our bodies and outside us with each other (no one fighting or arguing).

 Mindfulness Practice

Say: *Today we are going to start our class by having a Mindful Moment, just like last week. Who remembers what it means to get into our mindful bodies?*

Review the sequence of getting into our mindful bodies, noticing what's happening right now, listening to the bell until it stops, and then raising one hand. Practice these steps again if needed.

Say: *Okay, now that we remember what to do, let's have another Mindful Moment. Let's all get into our mindful bodies, close or cover our eyes, and notice what's happening right now. You may notice sounds inside the classroom, your breathing, or something else. We will tell what we noticed in a few moments after I ring the bell and we raise a hand. For now, we will continue to be quiet and just notice all that is happening right now….*

After a period of quiet, ring the bell, raise your hand when it stops, and open your eyes.

Ask: *Who would like to share what they noticed?*

Call on all students who raise their hands, and encourage with specific statements such as "that's amazing that you noticed a sound all the way out in the hallway" and "isn't it wonderful how much more we can notice when we're in our mindful bodies than in our regular bodies?"

 Lesson

Say: *Today we are going to learn how to do something that is pretty easy. In fact, you already know how to do it and actually are doing it <u>right now</u>. Tap your head if you know how to breathe.*

Everyone can tap their heads, because you've been breathing since the day you were born. You don't even need to think about your usual way of breathing because your body knows how to do it automatically.

But today we're going to learn about a special way to breathe called belly breathing. The air around us contains a chemical called oxygen. We can't smell it or see it, but it's there, and it's very good for our bodies. When we think about our breathing and do it very deeply, then we are getting oxygen deep into our bodies, from our bellies down to our toes. It feels really good to our bodies to get all this nice oxygen deep down inside. Are you ready to learn how to breathe deeply?

Show the picture of the flower or your artificial/real flower. Hold up one finger.

Say: *This finger is my pretend flower. Watch as I smell my flower very slowly (***bring your finger close to your face as you model this***) and notice how my belly goes out (***point to your extended belly***). Let's all try that together, and let's try to make our "sniff" last for four seconds. I'll count, ready? Let's all smell our flowers..2, 3, 4. Great job!*

Repeat several times as needed.

Say: *Now that we've breathed in all this great air and oxygen, what does our body need to do? Yes, blow it out! Here's how we do that when we're belly breathing.*

*Then I will softly blow the petals off my flower (***bring your finger toward your face as you slowly blow***) and notice how my belly goes in now.*

Model blowing as soft, quiet, and controlled. Some kids will want to make loud and noisy blows; just remind them to blow so quietly that others can't hear them.

Invite the children to practice this with you. Try to make the blows last four seconds, just like the sniffs. When everyone seems to understand the exercise, try it together as a group.

Say: *Now that we've got the hang of flowers and petals breathing, let's try it together. We'll smell our flowers and blow our petals three times. One hand will be our flowers, while the other hand can rest on our bellies as we feel them fill up with the air we breathe in, and then go soft again.* **Model placing one finger in front of you and your other hand on your belly**. *We will also try to make our breaths last for four seconds while I count. Are we ready? Here we go. Smell your flower, 2, 3, 4...and blow your petals, 2, 3, 4.* **Repeat for three breaths total**.

Say: *If we already know how to breathe, why do we need to know how to belly breathe?*

Facilitate a discussion on why it's good to know another way to breathe. Mainly because it <u>feels good to our bodies,</u> and helps us have that peaceful feeling discussed last week.

 Kindness Pals: Not introduced until Unit 2

Closing

Call on all students to name a time they can practice belly breathing during the week, at home or at school. Some suggestions may be when they are running and need to "catch their breath," before bedtime, or just alone in their rooms. Challenge each student to show another person how to belly breathe, too!

Say: *Try to practice your belly breathing with your flower at least once more this week, and we'll talk about it in our next **Peace of Mind** class. Have a great week!*

Optional Lesson Extensions:

Video - *Belly Breathe* by Sesame Street (widely available online at YouTube or other educational video websites). Have the children watch this short video featuring Elmo, Common, and Colbie Callait and practice belly breathing along with the characters in the song. *Warning, this is such a catchy tune and adorable video the students will beg for it again and again!*

Exercise – Have students stand up and run in place for 20-30 seconds, then place their hands on their hearts and notice how fast they are beating. Take three belly breaths together and then notice if anything feels different. Most will notice that their heart has slowed down.

Drawing – Give students blank paper folded in half. On one side they draw their flower they are pretending to smell, and on the other side they draw the same flower with some of the petals falling off to indicate blowing.

Book – *Take A Deep Breath* by Sue Graves. Read this book and have the students practice belly breathing along with the children in the story. Discuss how belly breathing helped the children in each scenario. Invite students to think of a time they might be able to use belly breathing to help them, too.

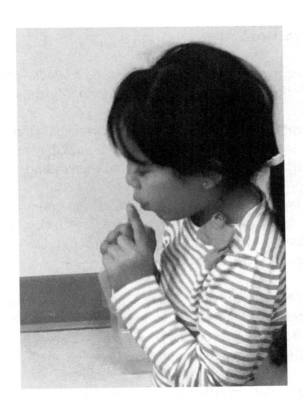

Week 3
Animal Breaths

OBJECTIVE: Bring attention to breaths; contrast shallow breaths and deep breaths.

> ASCA Standard:

B-SMS 2.
Demonstrate
self-discipline and
self-control

PREPARE: Bell or chime, puppet (optional: pictures or models of various animals)

Opening: *Hello again peaceful people! Did anyone practice your flower breathing during the week? If you did, I'd like to hear about it.*

Call on students to share their experiences practicing belly breaths during the week. Ask them to tell where they were when they practiced, and how they felt afterwards.

 Mindfulness Practice

Say: *Today we are going to start our class by having a Mindful Moment, just like last week. We will do this every time we have **Peace of Mind** class.*

Practice the steps for belly breathing with a flower again if needed. Then review the sequence of getting in our mindful bodies, paying attention to the moment, listening to the bell until it stops, and then raising a hand.

Say: *Okay, now that we remember what to do, let's have another Mindful Moment. We'll also use our belly breaths to get us started. Ready? Let's all get in our mindful bodies, close or cover our eyes, and take three deep belly breaths. Smell your flower…blow the petals….**Repeat twice more**.*

Notice what's happening right now. You may notice sounds inside the classroom, your breathing, or something else. We will tell what we noticed in a few moments after I ring the bell and we raise our hands. For now, we will continue to be quiet and just notice all that is happening right now.

After a period of quiet, ring the bell, raise your hand when it stops, and open your eyes.

Ask: *Who would like to share what they noticed?*

Call on all students who want to share, and give encouraging smiles, thumbs up, and other affirmations to all who share something.

 Lesson

Say: *I have a special friend who has been very excited to see you all again! Can you guess who it is? As soon as you get very quiet he will come out to say hello!*

Bring Paco out, panting and out of breath with his mouth wide open.

Puppet: *Hello again!* *(pant pant)* ***It's great to*** *(pant pant)* ***see you, class!***

Say: *Wow, does anyone notice something about Paco's breaths? Yes, they are very fast and loud. He's also breathing with his mouth open. That's called* <u>shallow or fast breathing</u>*. It's the opposite of our slow, deep belly breaths we just practiced.*

Invite the children to try breathing like Paco and notice how it feels. Ask if anyone has ever noticed themselves breathing like this, perhaps when running, angry, and so on. Explain the meaning of the word "shallow" using a pool as an analogy.

Say: *Something that's shallow, like water, means there's not very much of it. When something is deep, there's a lot of it. Our breaths can be described the same way. Paco has been running around and he doesn't have much breath. His breaths also aren't going very deep into his body, so that's why we can say they are shallow.*

Say: *Paco, you don't have much breath!*

Puppet: *Yes, I was running around a lot just before coming here and now my breaths are really fast and shallow.*

Say: *Can you think of a way to help Paco slow down his breathing and make it deeper? Yes, let's teach him how to belly breathe!*

Have the children model smelling their flower and blowing the petals to help Paco learn to belly breathe. Have Paco breathe in with his mouth closed, then breathe out with it open. Repeat this several times, then have Paco thank the children and return out of sight.

Say: *Thanks for helping Paco learn how to belly breathe! I notice that he's often breathing fast and shallow, like a lot of puppies do, because he runs around a lot. Let's think about some other animals and whether they breathe fast and shallow, or slow and deep.*

Lead a discussion on noticing and practicing how other animals move and breathe (deep and slow or fast and shallow). Here are some suggestions:

Slow and deep	Fast and shallow
Bears – curled up sleeping in the winter	Puppies – out for a walk, sniffing everything
Sea turtles – swimming slowly, rising up to the surface to take a deep breath	Rabbits – hopping around quickly
Snakes – slithering slowly, hissing	Butterflies – flitting about, landing on a flower, then flitting off again

Allow the children to practice being each kind of animal above, breathing slow and deep or fast and shallow as they do the movements in their place. If you want to allow moving about the room, plan for the activity to take a bit longer and use a quiet signal to gain attention and transition from one animal to the next.

> TEACHING TIP: Remember to practice your quiet signal from time to time. To practice using this signal have the children say "talk talk talk" and then stop when you shake the shaker (or use another signal). Do this a few times until everyone immediately gets quiet at the sound of the signal. Practice it now and again throughout the year.

Next, ask students to do the following:

Say: *That was amazing animal pretending! Show me with your hands how shallow or deep your breaths are right now.* Point your hands at your mouth (very shallow), neck, chest, or belly (very deep).

Note: There will be some variance, and that is fine. Try to come up with a general consensus that some breaths were deep and others were shallow.

 Kindness Pals: Not introduced until Unit 2

Closing: Invite students to share which animal breath they preferred from today's lesson. Model this by saying "My favorite animal breath was _____."

Say: *Try to practice your animal breaths again this week, and we'll talk about it in our next **Peace of Mind** class. See you next time!*

Optional Lesson Extension:

Activity – *Yoga Pretzels: 50 Fun Yoga Activities for Kids and Grownups*

Card deck by Leah Kalish and Tara Guber. Select several animal breaths from this deck and practice them with the children. Allow children to choose which animal breath they want to do for a Mindful Moment in between regular weekly practices.

Activity – *My Own Animal Breath* - Allow children to make up their own animal breath with an animal of their choosing. Let each child demonstrate the breath for the class, and show or tell where the breath is felt in the body (shallow or deep).

Week 4
Using My Body to Listen

OBJECTIVE: Bring awareness to various body parts that help us pay attention effectively.

PREPARE: Bell or chime, hand puppet

> ASCA Standard:

B-SMS 2.
Demonstrate self-discipline and self-control

Opening: *Hello, awesome amigos! Did anyone practice their belly breathing or animal breathing during the week?*

Call on students to share their experiences using one of the animal breaths from the last session, or belly breathing with their flowers. If someone introduces a new animal breath, have that student model it for the class.

Mindfulness Practice

Say: *How do you think we are going to begin our **Peace of Mind** class today? Yes, with our Mindful Moment of course! Today we will use our deep belly breathing again to start us off. We will do this every time we practice mindfulness together.*

Review the sequence of getting into mindful bodies, paying attention to the moment, listening to the bell until it stops, and raising a hand. Review belly breathing with flowers if needed.

Say: *Okay, now that we remember what to do, it's time for our Mindful Moment. Ready? Let's all get in our mindful bodies, close or cover our eyes, and take three deep belly breaths. Smell your flower…blow the petals***….Repeat twice more**.

Notice what's happening right now. You may notice sounds inside the classroom, your breathing, or something else. We will tell what we noticed in a few moments after I ring the bell and we raise our hands. For now, we will continue to be quiet and just notice all that is happening right now.

After a period of quiet, ring the bell, raise your hand when it stops, and open your eyes.

Ask: *Who would like to share what they noticed?*

Call on all students who raise their hands, affirming all who share something they noticed.

 Lesson

Say: *Today we're going to talk about and practice listening. When I say "listen," what part of your body do you think of using? Right, your ears! We definitely use those to listen. But did you know we can also use many other parts of our bodies to "hear" too? Let's think about how other parts besides our ears help us.*

Lead students through the following exercises for each body part. Establish your quiet signal that will mean it's time for that body part to listen.

Mouth

Say: *When mouths are making noise it's hard for ears to listen. Mouths help us listen by staying quiet when we're trying to hear something else.*

Invite the class to use their mouths by clicking tongues, talking, or making other noises. As it gets noisy, softly say a silly phrase like *I have three pink puppies in my bag.* Then give your quiet signal.

Say: *Now show me listening mouths. Who can tell me what I just said is in my bag?* Most of them will have no idea, but a few sitting near you may have heard and be able to tell the rest of the class part or all of your silly phrase. Repeat the phrase and point out how much better everyone can hear you with their listening mouths.

Hands

Say: *When hands are moving they usually make noise, and it's hard for ears to listen. Hands help us listen by staying still and quiet. Moving hands can sometimes be listening hands, as long as they are moving quietly and not disturbing or touching others.*

Invite the class to use their hands to clap, snap fingers, or make other motions. When it is noisy, softly say another silly phrase like *I have five green goblins in my bag.* Then give your quiet signal.

Say: *Now show me listening hands. Who heard me tell what is in my bag this time?* Most students will have no idea, but a few sitting near you may have heard and be able to tell the rest of the class your silly phrase. Repeat the phrase and point out how much better everyone can hear you with their listening hands.

> TEACHING TIP: Some will pick up on this "game" and try to both make noise and listen for your silly phrase at the same time. That's okay! Acting out the non-listening body parts is actually not the point of this activity anyway. Point out that they are able to hear your silly phrase because they are listening with their ears and bodies (good practice)! You can also make your voice softer to make it more challenging to hear you as needed.

Feet

Say: *When feet are moving they usually make noise, and it's hard for ears to listen. Feet help us listen by staying still and quiet. Moving feet can sometimes be okay, as long as they are moving quietly and not disturbing or touching others.*

Invite the class to use their feet to stomp, hop, or make other noisy motions. When it gets noisy, say another silly phrase like *I have twenty turquoise turtles in my bag*. Then give the quiet signal.

Say: *Now show me listening feet. Who heard what silly thing I said a moment ago?* Repeat the phrase and point out how much better everyone can hear you when their feet are listening.

Eyes

Say: *When eyes are moving they usually are looking at something, and it's hard for ears to listen when eyes are distracted by other things. Eyes help us listen by pointing at the person or thing we are listening to. Eyes can also help us hear when they are closed, as during the Mindful Moment when we're trying to listen to everything around us.*

Invite the class to use their eyes to turn and look all around the room. Say and motion another silly phrase like *I have (show a number on your fingers) scarlet slugs in my bag*. Then give the quiet signal.

Say: *Now show me listening eyes. Who knows what silly thing I have in my bag now?* Students will be able to name part of this, but may not have seen the number you showed on your fingers. Repeat the phrase and hand motion with everyone looking at you, and point out how much better everyone can hear you with their listening eyes.

Shoulders

Say: *When our shoulders are pointed away from what we're trying to listen to, it's hard for ears to hear. Shoulders help us listen by pointing toward the person or thing we are listening to.*

This time **you turn around with your back to the class**. Softly say another silly phrase like *I have one wiggly walrus in my bag*. Then turn back around to face the class.

Say: *Who heard what I said is in my bag this time? You couldn't hear me? Why ever not?* Of course, your own shoulders were not pointed at the class. Your shoulders weren't helping the class listen to you. Repeat the phrase while facing the class, and point out how much better everyone can hear each other with their listening shoulders.

> TEACHING TIP: Listening shoulders is an important concept to review throughout the year. From time to time, pull out the book you plan to read and turn your shoulders completely away from the class as you begin. When they laugh and ask what you are doing, say something like, "Oh, right! You can't listen to me very well with my shoulders turned away from you like that. I forgot! Thanks for the reminder. Now, I need all of YOU to remember the same thing and keep your shoulders pointed at me, too."

Others - Invite children to think of other parts of their bodies that help them listen. Some that might come up are arms, legs, fingers, toes, and brain. Let them model "listening arms" and so on, as time allows.

Say: *When we are using all those parts of our bodies, we can really listen and hear much better. That's like being in our mindful bodies at the beginning of Peace of Mind Class. When we are listening and paying attention with every part of ourselves, from head to toe, we will be amazed at everything we can listen to and notice happening around us!*

Kindness Pals: Not introduced until Unit 2

Closing: *Try to practice listening with all parts of your body this week, and we'll talk about it in our next **Peace of Mind** class. See you next time!*

Optional Lesson Extensions:

Video - *The Biscotti Kid* by Sesame Street (widely available online at YouTube or other educational video websites). Cookie monster has to listen with his whole body in order to earn his cookie belt. Show this short video to the class and discuss which parts he used and how.

Book - *Whole Body Listening Larry at School* by Elizabeth Sautter and Kristen Wilson. This rhyming story tells about teaching new students how to listen with their whole bodies. Read the story and pause to allow the children to guess each new body part. There is a poster that goes along with this book that can be used in class to remind kids how each part of their bodies can help them listen.

Week 5
What is Focus?

OBJECTIVE:	Apply previously-learned listening skills to experiment with and practice following instructions and maintaining focus during a group game.	> ASCA Standards: B-SMS 1. Demonstrate self-discipline and self-control
PREPARE:	Bell or chime, small "focus object" for each student to hold (pebble, marble, counter, penny, and so on)	B-SMS 4. Demonstrate ability to delay immediate gratification for long-term rewards

Opening: *Hello, fantastic friends! Last week we learned that many parts of our bodies can help us listen. Who noticed using part of your body to help you listen during the week?*

Call on students to share their experiences of using a body part to listen.

> TEACHING TIP: Even if students didn't remember the previous lesson at all, or didn't use the concepts throughout the week, the simple act of asking at the beginning of each class and allowing children to talk about it will foster greater recall and potential use throughout the next week as students become used to the routine of starting each class by talking about the previous one.

Mindfulness Practice

Say: *Let's check in with those body parts as we get ready for our Mindful Moment. Now let's start with our feet...are they listening? Our legs....our hands....our mouths...and our ears.... Try to notice if each part is helping you listen as we start* **Peace of Mind** *class now. Today during our Mindful Moment we will try to focus our attention on just our bodies and breaths.*

Review the sequence of getting into mindful bodies, paying attention to the moment, listening to the bell until it stops, and then raising a hand. Review belly breathing with flowers and petals. Practice these steps again if needed.

Say: *Ready? Let's all get in our mindful bodies, close or cover our eyes, and take three deep belly breaths. Smell your flower...blow the petals....***Repeat twice more***.

Notice what's happening right now. You may notice sounds inside the classroom, your breathing, or something else. We will tell what we noticed in a few moments after I ring the bell and we raise our hands. For now, we will continue to be quiet and just notice all that is happening right now.

After a period of quiet, ring the bell, raise your hand when it stops, and open your eyes.

Ask: *Who would like to share what they noticed about their bodies and breaths?*

Call on all students who raise their hands, and give affirmations to all who share something.

 Lesson

Say: *Today during our Mindful Moment I asked you to <u>focus</u> on your body and breaths. What do you think the word <u>focus</u> means?*

Take a few suggestions and then give the following simple definition: focus means to see clearly, or to pay close attention to something.

Say: *Often grown-ups tell kids to "focus," but we sometimes forget to teach you HOW to focus. To help you learn how to focus, or pay really close attention to something, we are going to play a fun game called "Don't Lose Your Focus!"*

Explain that during our game students will get their very own "focus object" to hold in their hands. This is what they will focus on during the game. The rules of the game are simple, but require them to listen carefully to all of the directions. Remind them they can use their <u>bodies</u> to help them listen right now. If they don't hear all of the directions, they might miss something and not be able to play the game.

> TEACHING TIP: Based The Concentration Circle by artist Sean Layne, "Don't Lose Your Focus" helps young children practice keeping their focus on one thing. When playing with very young children, the expectation is not complete stillness and silence. Rather, look to see that children are making attempts to stand quietly and still, and most importantly are attempting to ignore the planned distractions. This is the real value in the game.

Explain the following instructions to the class.

Don't Lose Your Focus! Game instructions:

1. Ask students stand in a large circle facing in, not touching.

2. Tell them that when they hear the word "Go!" they must freeze their bodies like a statue, with their hands cupped in front of them.

3. Breathing and blinking are fine, but they must try very hard to remain still and silent. Explain that mindful breathing can help you keep your focus!

4. Students should focus on (look intently at) the object that will be placed in their cupped hands, but they should try to resist the temptation to play with their objects or move them around. Just ask them to try to let them lie in their hands.

5. If they move a lot, look around, laugh, talk, or play with their object, remove it from their hands. They "lost their focus."

6. As soon as they regain their focus (quiet, still body with hands cupped in front), return the object to them.

After reviewing these instructions, invite students to stand up. Have them shake and wiggle for a moment, since they will be standing very still until everyone has their focus (object in their hand). Although some may still have questions, as long as they understand steps 1 and 2 they will quickly get the rest as you begin to play. You can also quietly give reminders as you move around the circle during the game.

Give a countdown: *5, 4, 3, 2, 1, Focus!*

Walk around the inside of the circle, placing an object in the cupped hands of each student who is still and quiet. Remind them to focus on (look closely at) their object but not play with it. Remove objects from students who do so, quickly returning them as soon as the student gets still again. It should take no more than five minutes for everyone to have their objects (having lost and re-earned several times). After everyone has their objects,

Say: *We have passed Level 1 of this game! You can now <u>unfreeze</u> and sit down right where you are!*

Have everyone sit in the circle, and tell them they can now touch and gently play with the object in their hand. Congratulate them on having great body listening and focus. Ask students who did not lose their object to share how they were able to remain so still and resist temptation to play with their objects. Explain that this game has several levels:

Level 1 - Everyone earns their object, and all have it at the same time.

Level 2 - Everyone is able to focus on their object while you (the teacher) are making a silly face in front of them.

Level 3 - Everyone is able to focus on their object while the puppet is making silly gestures/acting crazy in front of them.

Level 4 - Everyone is able to focus on their object when a classmate makes a silly face or somehow tries to distract them.

Level 5 - Everyone is able to focus on their object when a song or video is playing nearby.

> TEACHING TIP: A good expectation for the first time this game is played is to complete Level 3. Once the children get the hang of it they will request this game again and again! If you have even three minutes to spare at the end of a class, you can announce there is time to play Don't Lose Your Focus and begin the countdown. Kids will scramble to get

in position and be ready when you say "Focus!" Always start over with Level 1 before moving through each level sequentially. On some days classes will be able to make it through the levels quicker than on others, which is fine.

After reaching Level 3 or running out of time, collect the objects and use your quiet signal.

Facilitate a discussion on how everyone was able to _focus_ themselves in such a still and quiet manner for the length of the game. Discuss some or all of the following questions:

1. Has anyone ever told you to "focus" before?
2. Did they show you how to do it?
3. When are times we need to focus in school?
4. How does it help us to be able to focus in school?
5. How does Mindful Breathing help you to focus?
6. When your teacher is in front of the class talking, can you make them your focus object?

7. When you are working on something at your seat, can you make your work the focus object?

8. How were you able to ignore distractions? Can you do the same thing when you are focusing in school?

9. The next time you notice you're having trouble focusing in school, can you practice your mindful breathing and then pretend to play this game with yourself, making your teacher or work the object of your focus?

> TEACHING TIP: This game is meant to be repeated, so these questions can also be asked at later times. It can be helpful to remind students of this game from time to time even if you don't play it: "Right now let's remember our Focus game, and make me your focus object. Try to ignore distractions around you as you stay focused on me."

 Kindness Pals: Not introduced until Unit 2

Closing: *Try to practice focusing on a specific thing, like your teacher or your work, and we'll talk about it in our next **Peace of Mind** class. See you next time!*

Optional Lesson Extensions:

Video – *Cookies of the Caribbean* by Sesame Street. Show this short video in which Cookie Monster must focus and not give up when trying to reach Davy Jones' cookie jar.

Credit *to Sean Layne, Founder of Focus, 5, Inc.* *www.ArtsIntegrationConsulting.com*

Unit 2
Mindful of My Feelings and Thoughts

Mindfulness Skills –
Noticing Emotions, Noticing Thoughts

Target quiet time during mindfulness ≅ 30 seconds

Week 6
New Friends and Kindness Pals

OBJECTIVES: Demonstrate the purpose and routine of Kindness Pals; practice basic communication skills of facing, greeting, speaking, and listening.

PREPARE: Bell or chime, pre-made Kindness Pal list (see Appendix for template)

> ASCA Standards:

B-SS 1. Use effective oral . . . communication skills and listening skills

B-SS 2. Create positive and supportive relationships with other students

TEACHING TIP: Today's mindfulness script will mention feelings. Because the concept of feelings and emotions is not formally introduced until Week 7, consider this an informal pre-assessment of your students' familiarity with the concepts and vocabulary around feelings and emotions.

Opening: *Hello, wonderful wizards! Who noticed yourself <u>focusing</u> on something like we did in the game last time? Did you use your mindful breathing to help you focus on a story your teacher was reading, or a drawing you were doing, or something else?*

Call on students who have something to share about focusing their attention.

 Mindfulness Practice

Say: *Today during our Mindful Moment we are going to focus on, or pay close attention to, any feelings we notice in our bodies. Try to pay attention to your body and how it is feeling right now.*

*Ready? Let's all get in our mindful bodies, close or cover our eyes, and take three deep belly breaths. Smell your flower…blow the petals….***Repeat twice more***.*

Notice what's happening right now. You may notice sounds inside the classroom, your breathing, or something else. We will tell what we noticed in a few moments after I ring the bell and we raise our hands. For now, we will continue to be quiet and notice our bodies….

After a period of quiet, ring the bell, raise your hand when it stops, and open your eyes.

> TEACHING TIP: It can be very useful to count seconds to yourself to monitor the amount of time between your final words and the bell ringing. The "target quiet time" listed for each Unit is a suggested time based on typical development of young children, but can always be adjusted for specific classroom needs. It can be hard to gauge how much time has passed if you do not count.

Ask: *Who would like to share something you noticed in your body?*

Call on all students who raise their hands and give affirmations to all who share something, even if it is not a feeling or body related. Many will likely still name sounds they heard.

 Lesson

Say: *Today we are going to start practicing kindness. When we practice something, we get better at it. We are going to practice kindness every time we have **Peace of Mind** class from now on!*

Ask students to share something they practiced a lot and then got better at. Explain that being kind works the same way. The more we practice, the easier it gets for us, too.

Say: *To help us practice kindness, each student in the class is going to get a Kindness Pal, someone else in your class that I've matched you up with. In each **Peace of Mind** class we have from now on, we will work with our Kindness Pals. However, before I give you your first Kindness Pal, there are a few things we need to practice.*

Skill 1: **Responding with "Okay" and a smile**

Say: *In just a minute, I will call out two names, and those students I call will be each other's Kindness Pal. The first thing they need to do is look at each other, smile, and say "Okay!"* Model this by saying your name and a student name for practice. *So, _____ and (your name) are going to be Kindness Pals.*

Turn to the student, smile and say *Okay!* Make sure the student says "okay."

Skill 2: How to face each other

Say: *After I call out all the pals, you will move to sit next to each other and you will face each other. To face each other just means your faces are looking at each other.*

Turn to one student and point your face at that student. Then let your attention and face wander away and ask the students if you are still facing your "pal." Turn your face back to the student and emphasize this is how we face each other.

Skill 3: The Kindness Pal listening position

Say: *When you sit near your pal and face each other, you will also need to crisscross your legs, line your knees up with each other so they are almost touching, and make sure your shoulders are pointed at each other. You will need to use your whole body to listen to your pal!* You may want to use two nearby children, or yourself and another child, to model this for the class.

Once you've established these expectations you are ready to start the first Kindness Pal session.

TEACHING TIPS ON KINDNESS PALS:

- Since this is the first lesson where Kindness Pals (KP) take place it's important to make sure everyone is able to work with a teacher-assigned partner. If you are not the children's classroom teacher, it may be helpful to ask for input on the pairings.

- Initially very young children will not have any problems saying "okay!" enthusiastically when they hear the name of their KP. However, after they get more used to this activity and have formed closer friendships within the class, you may experience some resistance or requests for their "best friend" to be their assigned KP. If this happens, remind children they can keep any thoughts about who they would rather have inside their thought bubbles (a concept presented in Week 9) , and do not need to say it aloud. You can use the puppet to model saying something like "Oh, I really wanted ___ to be my pal instead of (your own name)" and explain how that makes you feel to know Paco didn't want to be your pal.

- Very rarely, some children might get upset and cry over their pal assignment. If that occurs, quickly assign the pal to join another group and form a threesome, finish calling out all the pals, and then gently talk individually with the child who is crying to help him understand he is not being kind to his new pal. Remind him, and the whole class periodically, that he can still be friends with anyone in the class he wants to at recess and other free times. His Kindness Pal doesn't have to be a friend, but is another person to be kind to. The KP does not replace all the friends that children already have or would like to have. When he is ready, he can join the threesome and continue the activity as a group of four.

 ## Kindness Pals

Call out each pair of Kindness Pals from your list, wait for both students to say "Okay," notice and comment when they give each other big smiles, and help them decide who should move near whom. Make sure they are in a good listening position as described above.

Once all children have been matched up and any absences accounted for, remind them all to listen for the quiet signal when they are chatting with their pal, as that will mean it's time to stop talking and listen for the next directions.

Say: *The first thing we will always do with our pal is to give each other a friendly greeting. A friendly greeting could be a high five, a handshake, a "hello, how are you?" or a fist bump. It could be all of those things. Ready? Go ahead and give your new pal some kind greetings right now!*

Allow time for greetings, then use your quiet signal.

Say: *I saw some wonderfully friendly and kind greetings! Now we are going to talk about some of our favorite things with our pal. Today we will tell our favorite colors and foods. Go ahead.*

After a couple minutes, give the quiet signal again.

Say: *I'd like to find out if you and your pal had anything in common. That means you both like the same favorite things. If you and your pal had something in common, put both hands on your head.*

Allow students to share out what they had in common, calling on pals as a unit rather than individually.

Say: *Our time is almost up for today. The last thing you are going to do with your Kindness Pal is give each other a friendly goodbye. That could be a wave, a "see you later," another fist bump or high five, and then return to your seats.*

Explain that you will <u>leave the Kindness Pal list posted in the classroom</u> and that the pal names are listed beside each other. If they forget who their pals are during the week they can find the names on the list and try to figure out whose name is next to theirs. Or they may ask a teacher as reading levels vary widely at this stage.

Closing: *Try to remember to do something kind for your new Kindness Pal, and tell me about it in our next* **Peace of Mind** *class. See you then!*

Optional Lesson Extensions:

Books – There are many simple picture books on kindness, including the lovely series from Carol McCloud, *Have You Filled A Bucket Today?* Read these or other similar-themed books to the students as they sit with their new Kindness Pals. They can "fill a bucket" for their pal by giving smiles and other kind greetings to each other.

Drawing – Allow students to make a drawing for their new Kindness Pal and exchange them with each other afterwards.

Classwork Partners – Use Kindness Pals to partner students throughout the week during various learning activities.

Week 7
Noticing My Feelings

OBJECTIVES:	Attend to feelings; identify, define, and act out at least five basic feelings words.	> ASCA Standards: B-SS 1. Use effective oral and written communication skills and listening skills B-SS 2. Create positive and supportive relationships with other students
PREPARE:	Bell or chime, puppet	

Say: *Hello, class! Does anyone remember who their Kindness Pal is? Were you kind to your Kindness Pal during the week? Let's do a quick check-in to see who remembers their pal.*

Ask children to give a thumbs up if they definitely know who their assigned pals are, a thumb in the middle if they think they know but aren't sure, and a thumbs down if they do not remember at all. All are okay!

> TEACHING TIP: Children love to share their thoughts with the teacher. The more you can incorporate ways to have everyone "tell" something at the same time, the less frustration there will be all around. Using hands to model any kind of nonverbal response is easy and effective, as is allowing everyone to say an obvious word or answer aloud in unison. Use different voices to make it more interesting: whisper, sing, high voice, low voice, and so on.

Mindfulness Practice

Say: *Today during our Mindful Moment and **Peace of Mind** class we are going to talk about and notice feelings we have in our bodies again. Try to pay attention to your body and how it is feeling right now. Is it tired? Happy? Full of energy? Or perhaps something else? In a few minutes we will try to name as many feelings as we can think of.*

*Now it's time for us to get in our mindful bodies, close or cover our eyes, and take three deep belly breaths. Smell your flower...blow the petals....**Repeat twice more**.*

Notice what's happening right now. You may notice sounds inside the classroom, your breathing, or something else. We will tell what we noticed in a few moments after I ring the bell and we raise our hands. For now, we will continue to be quiet and just notice all that is happening right now.

TEACHING TIP: Occasionally remind students to keep what they notice inside their minds and not say it out loud until after the Mindful Moment is over and it's time to share. This will take some getting used to for some children.

After a period of quiet, ring the bell, raise your hand when it stops, and open your eyes.

Ask: *Who would like to share a feeling you noticed in your body?*

Call on all students who raise a hand and give affirmations to all who share something, even if it is not a feeling.

 Lesson

Say: *You are beginning to notice your feelings, everyone. Now we're going to talk a little more about all the many different feelings there are. Let's get Paco to help us, okay?*

Bring out Paco once everyone is quiet. Today he is feeling shy and hides behind you.

Say: *Paco, say hello to the children. They are so excited to see you again!* Coax him to come out. Have him peek at the kids, then whisper in your ear. *What's that? You're having a feeling?*

Ask the children if they know what a feeling is, and what it has to do with Paco. They will probably be able to guess that a feeling is something like happy or sad, and that Paco is feeling shy, scared, or nervous.

Say: *Yes, Paco told me he is feeling a little shy today to see all of you again. But Paco, remember you met these very nice kids several times already and have had so much fun with them! Look at how quietly they are sitting so they don't frighten you.* Have Paco peek at the children, then look more closely at them. Finally, he can speak quietly.

Puppet: Oh, *that's right, I did meet you all before! Well, today I felt very shy and nervous about coming here and seeing you again. It can be a little scary to get up in front of a whole class and talk sometimes. But I'm already starting to feel a little happier and less nervous!*

Explain that a <u>feeling</u> is something that happens inside our bodies, also called an emotion, and we usually show it on our faces and in our actions, too. Our feelings can change many times throughout the day. Some feelings bring smiles and energy, like happiness and excitement, while others bring frowns, like sadness or anger. Emphasize that feelings aren't right or wrong, and one feeling isn't better than another. We all have lots of different feelings each day. Point out how Paco's feelings changed from nervous to calm or happy just now.

Say: *Paco, we are going to talk about some of the many feelings we have, and I was hoping the children would help model those feelings on their faces and bodies, and you would tell us a time you had each feeling, so we are sure we know what they mean.*

Puppet: *Okay, I'm feeling great now that I remember all these kids and would love to model some feelings with them! What's the first one?*

Ask students to name as many feelings words they can think of. These will usually include basics like happy, sad, and mad. Then use the following list for you (not the puppet) to model the feelings, and the class to copy you, with faces and bodies. Depending on your puppet's style he will mostly add context comments for each feeling. Go through as many of these, or others the students think of, as you have time for.

- Happy – smile, eyes open wide, and shoulders raised a bit (Paco: ***Like when I find a new bone to eat!***)

- Scared – straight face, eyes open wide, arms folded in a defensive position (Paco: ***Like when it storms outside and I hide under the bed.***)

- Angry or mad – eyes narrowed, mouth turned down, fast breaths, hands balled in fists (Paco: ***Like that time I couldn't have two desserts after dinner.***)

- Excited – big smile, open mouth, eyebrows raised (Paco: ***Like the time I <u>did</u> get to have two desserts after dinner!***)

- Sad – frown, eyes look down, shoulders slumped (Paco: ***Like when I lost my collar.***)

- Overjoyed – big smile, hands above head in a cheering position (Paco: ***Like when I came in first place in a race!***)

- Terrified – mouth open in a silent scream, eyes wide, fast breaths, (Paco: ***Like the time I thought I saw a snake outside only it really was just a stick***!)

- Tired – yawn, stretch, close eyes (Paco: ***Like when I stay up late to watch a movie.***)

- Loving – smile, give self a hug (Paco: *Like when I hug my mom/dad/ grandma.*)

- Disgusted – wrinkle nose, frown, say "ugh" or "yuck" (Paco: *Like when my dad fixes something for supper I don't like!*)

- Worried – forehead wrinkled, slight frown, eyes dart around (Paco: *Like the time I thought we were late for school.*)

- Grumpy – lips pooch out, eyes down, say "humph!" (Paco*: Like when I don't want to wake up in the morning.*)

- Shy – drawn in face, eyes look away (Paco: *Like when I didn't want to come out to see everyone today!*)

- Calm – take a deep breath, slight smile, eyes closing, say "ahh" (Paco: *Like when we have our Mindful Moment.*)

Say: *These are just some of the many feelings there are. We get different feelings all the time, often because of something happening at the moment. We usually show our feelings on our faces and in our bodies. Our feelings also change often, and we can even have more than one feeling in our bodies at the same time.*

 Kindness Pals

Say: *Who's ready to practice kindness again today? We'll be working with the same pal as last week. Remember that when I call your names your job is to smile at each other, say "Okay," and move to sit near each other in a good listening position.*

Call out each pair of Kindness Pals from your list, wait for both students to say "Okay," notice and comment when they give each other big smiles, and help them decide who should move near whom. Make sure they are in a good listening position as described above. Remind them not to start talking yet.

> TEACHING TIP: Pals will almost always be excited to begin chatting to one another, often as soon as they move to sit next to each other. Remember that getting to move out of your assigned seat and talk freely to another student is such a novel activity for little ones! Gently remind the students that in order for everyone else to hear their pal's name called, everyone must be quiet until all pals are matched up. If particular classes or individual students continue to struggle with this, consider having them wait to move next to each other until all names are called and instructions for KP time have been given.

When two or more students are absent, pair their KPs with each other. If only one student is absent, pair that student's KP with another group to form a threesome. Once all children have been matched up and any absences accounted for, remind all groups to listen for the quiet signal when they are chatting with their pal, as that will mean it's time to stop talking and listen for the next directions.

Say: *Remember, the first thing we will always do with our pal is to give each other a friendly greeting. A friendly greeting could be a high five, a handshake, a "hello, how are you?" a fist bump, or all of those things. Ready? Go ahead and give your new pal some kind greetings right now!*

Allow some time to give greetings.

Say: *Now we are going to talk about feelings with our pal. I'll name one of the feelings we just talked about, and you will tell about a time you had that feeling and what you were doing when you had it. Decide which pal will talk first while the other listens, then switch so that the other pal gets a chance to talk while the first one listens. If you both finish talking and I still have not given the quiet signal, you can each tell about a different time you had that same feeling. Ready? The first feeling you will talk about is _____.* Name one from your discussion, other than "happy" and "sad."

As the pals begin talking move around the room to listen to their conversations. You can also use this time to adjust listening positions as needed, help students who can't think of something to say, and to gauge when everyone is more or less finished sharing.

Use the quiet signal and give another feeling. Try to allow pals to talk about at least five different feelings before you instruct them to say goodbye and move back to their seats.

Closing: *Try to notice any feelings you are having this week, and tell me about it in our next **Peace of Mind** class. See you then!*

Optional Lesson Extensions:

Books – There are many good picture books about feelings, such as *Glad Monster, Sad Monster* by Ed Emberly and Anne Miranda; *Today I Feel Silly* by Jamie Lee Curtis; and *My Many-Colored Days* by Dr. Suess. Choose one or more to read to the class, having students use picture cues to guess the feeling on each page before you read it.

Games – Use feelings flashcards, such as Todd Parr's Feelings Flashcards box, to play feelings charades. Secretly show the picture to a student and have him act it out in front of the class. Take turns until everyone who wants to act has had a chance to do so.

Week 8
Feelings Can Be Different Sizes

		> ASCA Standards:
OBJECTIVES:	Identify feelings as small, medium or large using a 5-point scale; define "calming down" as moving from a higher number to a lower number on the feelings thermometer; use deep breathing as a way to calm down.	B-SMS 1. Demonstrate ability to assume responsibility
PREPARE:	Bell or chime, puppet, thermometer picture (see Appendix) or real classroom thermometer relabeled with numbers 1-5	B-LS 4. Apply self-motivation and self-direction to learning

Opening: *Hello again peaceful people! Last week we learned about many different feelings in* **Peace of Mind** *class. Did anyone notice a feeling you were having this week?*

Call on students to share. Since almost everyone can have a feeling word to share, consider going around in a circle and calling on each student to name a feeling.

 Mindfulness Practice

Say: *Today we are going to continue talking about our feelings. During our Mindful Moment we are going to focus on, or notice, any feelings in our bodies. Does something feel sad, or glad, or tired, or excited? Try to notice these or other feelings in your body.*

Now it's time for us to get in our mindful bodies, close or cover our eyes, and take three deep belly breaths. Smell your flower…blow the petals….**Repeat twice more**.

Notice what's happening right now. You may notice sounds inside the classroom, your breathing, or something else. We will tell what we noticed in a few moments after I ring the bell and we raise our hands. For now, we will continue to be quiet and just notice all that is happening right now.

After a period of quiet, ring the bell, raise your hand when it stops, and open your eyes.

Ask: *Who would like to name a feeling you noticed right now in your body?*

Call on all students who raise their hands and give affirmations to all who share.

> TEACHING TIP: If possible allow time each week for students to tell about using their mindful breathing or other *Peace of Mind* skills at home, on the weekends, and at school outside of your class. This is a great way to reinforce the idea that these are life skills to be used any time, not just during *Peace of Mind* class!

 Lesson

Show the thermometer to the class, and ask for students to guess what it is used for. Eventually guide them to the simple answer: measuring how hot or cold something is.

Explain that we can also use this tool to measure the size of our feelings, too. Point to the numbers 1-5 on your thermometer as you explain the following system:

1 = Calm, cool, our "usual self"

2 = A small feeling is noticed, like a shoe bothering you or needing water.

3 = A feeling is getting bigger or heating up, and is starting to bother you more.

4 = A feeling is getting hotter, taking up your whole body, and you may start crying.

5 = A feeling becomes too big for your body and explodes out. This usually looks like a tantrum or meltdown of some sort.

Use Paco to demonstrate the 1-5 feelings thermometer. Today he will tell a story about going to the veterinarian's office to get a shot, something many children can relate to as a fear-inducing activity.

> TEACHING TIP: If there are children in the class with specific phobias or of a very fearful nature, you may want to consider using a different story that has near-universal big feelings other than fear, such anger resulting from losing or breaking a favorite toy.

Say: *Paco, you have a story about a number 5 feeling, and I'd like you to tell it to the class.*

Puppet: *Oh, you mean that time I had to get a...you know what? Okay, here's what happened. I was at home, on a Saturday morning, watching my favorite cartoons. I was at a 1, feeling cool and calm. Then, my mom said "Paco, we have to go to the vet's office today." I thought, hmm, why are we going to the vet on a Saturday? I was a little worried. My feelings were at a 2. Mommy, why do I have to go to the vet? I'm not getting a shot, am I?*

Just the thought of having to get a shot put me up to a 3! I HATE shots! And you know what she said? "Yes, Paco, you have to get a shot today." Ohhhh no! Now my feeling was a 4. I started whimpering and crying a little. Please no, Mommy, I don't want to get a shot today! But we had to get in the car and drive to the vet's office. I resisted going in, but my mom pulled me inside. I sat and cried until it was time to go in the exam room. The vet got out the needle, came over to me, and that's when it happened. My feelings went to a 5!

Here have Paco zoom around screaming and yelling, fall down on the floor, and act really out of control. Use your quiet signal as needed to get the kids to settle down, as they will find this very funny and may get out of control themselves!

> TEACHING TIP: This topic will almost certainly inspire children to want tell their own experiences with getting a shot. If so, let them know that during today's Kindness Pal time each child will get to tell a story about a time they had a big feeling.

Ask: *Who can name some of the feelings Paco was having on that day?* (Fear, afraid, terrified, nervous, and so on.)

Thank Paco for telling his story and put him away.

Tell the rest of the story, which is that Paco was able to quickly calm down after he got his shot, and the shot didn't hurt nearly as badly as he thought it would. He took some deep belly breaths with his mom's help. She gave him a big hug, and told him he could watch cartoons again when they got home. When they left the vet's office he was at a 3, and pretty soon he was back home again watching his cartoons and back at a 1, calm and cool.

Say: *When we have a size 4 or 5 feeling and we are able to bring it back down to a 1, 2, or 3 sized feeling, we call it calming down. Has anyone ever told you to "calm down?" They probably noticed you having a big feeling and were telling you to try to get the feeling to be a little smaller. Grown-ups often tell kids to calm down, but forget to show them how to do that!*

Remind students that they will share their own big-sized feelings stories, along with how they calmed down, in a few minutes during Kindness Pals.

Ask: *How was Paco able to calm down after his shot?* Belly breathing, thinking about cartoons, getting a hug from his mom, and so on.

Ask: *What might have happened if Paco had taken some deep belly breaths in the car on the way to the vet's office, and thought about his cartoons inside the office, instead of waiting until after the shot was over.* He might have stayed at a 3 or a 4 instead of having the huge 5-sized feeling in the vet's office!

 Kindness Pals

Say: *Who's ready to practice kindness again today? We'll be working with the same pals as last week, and today you will each take a turn to talk about a time you had a big feeling. Remember that when I call your names your job is to smile at each other, say "Okay," and move to sit near each other in a good listening position.*

Call out each pair of Kindness Pals from your list, wait for both students to say "Okay," notice and comment when they give each other big smiles, and help them decide who should move near whom. Account for any absences as before.

Say: *Remember, the first thing we will always do with our pals is to give each other a friendly greeting. A friendly greeting could be a high five, a handshake, a "hello, how are you?", a fist bump, or all of those things. Ready? Go ahead and give your new pal some kind greetings right now!*

Give the quiet signal, then say: *Now we are going to talk about a time you had a big "number 5-sized" feeling. What happened? How did you act? How did you go back to a 1 again, or calm down? Decide which pal will talk first while the other listens, then switch so that the other pal gets a chance to talk while the first one listens. If you both finish talking and I still have not given the quiet signal, you can each tell about another time you had a big feeling. Go ahead.*

Move around the room as the pals begin talking to listen to their conversations. You can also use this time to adjust listening positions as needed, help students who can't think of something to say, and to gauge when everyone is more or less finished sharing.

When most students are finished sharing, say: *Our time is almost up for today. The last thing you are going to do with your Kindness Pal is give each other* *a friendly goodbye. That could be a wave, a "see you later," or another high five and then return to your seats.*

Say: *We are going to all put up our fingers to show how we are feeling right now at the end of* **Peace of Mind** *class. If you're relaxed and calm you will hold up one finger (model holding up your fingers), if you have a small feeling you notice in your body, hold up two fingers, if you have a bigger feeling hold up three fingers.*

Point out that no one is out of control of their bodies or crying (hopefully), so likely no one has a feeling that's a size 4 or 5. Most children will feel like a 1, 2, or 3. Look around the room at everyone's number and informally assess how well they grasped this concept.

Closing: *Try to notice any big, 4 or 5-sized feelings you are having this week, and what helps you calm down to a smaller feeling. See you next time, class!*

Optional Lesson Extensions:

Video – Now is a great time to allow students to re-watch the Sesame Street video *Belly Breathe*. Ask what feeling Elmo was having (anger), and label this as a 5. Point out how he was able to "feel like himself again" after belly breathing and get back to a 1.

Book - *When My Worries Get Too Big* by Kari Dunn Buron. This shows a child going through the 5-point scale and the strategies he uses to get back to a 1. Read this and have the children follow along with his strategies, pretending to calm themselves. This book also contains several sample 1-5 scales for reference, which can be useful for individual children to complete.

Credit: *Buron, K. D., & Curtis, M. (2012). The Incredible 5-point Scale: The Significantly Improved and Expanded Second Edition: Assisting Students in Understanding Social Interactions and Controlling Their Emotional Responses. Shawnee Mission, KS: AAPC Inc.*

Week 9
My Thoughts and Thought Bubbles

OBJECTIVES: Explore concepts of thoughts and thought bubbles; make use of a thought bubble illustration to show something one is thinking about.

PREPARE: Bell or chime, puppet, 1 thought bubble page per student (see Appendix), new Kindness Pal list

> ASCA Standards:

B-LS 2. Demonstrate creativity

B-SS 2. Create positive and supportive relationships with other students

Opening: *Hello class! Did anyone notice any big feelings since we last met? Were you able to use your flower and petals breathing (or something else) to help you calm down?*

Call on several students who want to share.

 Mindfulness Practice

Say: *Thoughts and feelings usually go together. They happen at the same time in our bodies. Today we're going to be talking about and noticing our thoughts. Who knows what a thought is?*

Define a thought as something we are thinking about inside our brain.

Say: *During our Mindful Moment today we are going to try to notice the thoughts we are having in our brains. Pay attention to what's going on in your brain. Are you thinking about your breathing? Are you thinking about sounds you hear in the class when it's very quiet? Are you thinking about something that happened earlier today, something you want to do later today, or something imaginary? All of these are <u>thoughts</u>, and all of them are perfectly fine to be having.*

*Now it's time for us to get in our mindful bodies, close or cover our eyes, and take three deep belly breaths. Smell your flower…blow the petals.…**Repeat twice more**.*

Notice what's happening right now. You may notice sounds inside the classroom, your breathing, or something else. We will tell what we noticed in a few moments after I ring the bell and we raise our hands. For now, we will continue to be quiet and just notice all that is happening right now.

After a period of quiet, ring the bell, raise your hand when it stops, and open your eyes.

Ask: *Who would like to share a thought you noticed?*

Call on all students who raise their hands and give affirmations to all who share, even if their comments are not about a thought.

> TEACHING TIP: Sometimes when children share, they can get off topic and the next person will follow that lead. It can be helpful to state explicitly what you want to know each time you call on someone. For example, "What were you thinking about, Timmy?" "And what were you thinking about, Janae?" and so on to remind each child what was asked and help stay on topic.

 Lesson

Say: *Class, Paco really wants to see you today. I'm going to let him come talk to you right now.*

Today Paco is zooming all around, super excited, and talking very loud and fast, and panting in between his words. The children will first review calming down by taking belly breaths, and then further explore his thoughts to see what's making him so excited. Paco speaks loudly and quickly.

Puppet: *Oh wow, oh wow, I'm really glad to see you all again I have so much to tell you I've had such a great adventure and I had so much fun and I....(pant pant pant).*

Say: *Paco, buddy, you really have to calm down a little so we can understand you and hear everything you're trying to say!*

Puppet: *Oh no, I forgot what it means to "calm down." How do I calm down?*

Review calming down as moving from a higher number to a lower number on the feelings thermometer. Ask if anyone can name Paco's feeling (excited, super happy, elated) and give it a number (a 3 or 4 because he's almost out of control).

Ask the children if anyone can explain to Paco what it means to calm down and give him some ideas on what he can do. When someone says "belly breathing," have the whole class model it for Paco while he copies them again.

Squeeze the puppet's mouth together and pull back to indicate breathing in, open the mouth widely and lean forward to indicate breathing out.

After taking three breaths, Paco is calmer and now speaks more slowly.

Puppet: *Thank you so much. I don't have that jumpy feeling inside anymore, and I feel much calmer, so I guess that's what it means to <u>calm down</u>. Now I can tell you why I'm so excited today! You see, I went on an adventure yesterday and found my favorite thing in the whole world...bones! I just can't stop thinking about all those yummy bones I found on my trip. I dug up the most delicious bones ever! Oooh, just thinking about all those bones makes me feel really happy!*

Ask: *If we could see what Paco is thinking about right now, what would it be? That's right, bones! Do you know what part of our bodies we use for thinking? Yes, our brains, which are inside our heads. To show what people are thinking in their brains in books and stories, we use a thought bubble that looks like this.*

Put Paco down on your lap and show one of the thought bubble pages. Point out the bumpy edges, like a cloud, and the smaller bubbles leading to your head. Hold it over Paco's head and draw a simple bone inside. Point out that Paco feels really happy when he thinks about his bones. Just like Paco, our thoughts and feelings go together. We feel happy when we think about our favorite things or people. We may also feel sad or scared if we think about other things.

Distribute a blank page to each student, with instructions to draw something that makes them feel very happy when they think of it, like Paco with his bones.

Some students may be able to draw a different thought and feeling that go together besides the happy one. For example, feeling sad when they think about a lost toy.

> TEACHING TIPS: This will be the first class where students create something and share it with the group (share = tell about their picture briefly), so it will be important to set expectations and a routine for how you will share out when everyone has a drawing. This will prevent the natural tendency to play with their papers, roll them up, and/or talk to each other. Consider using one of the following ways to share. These options are organized from least to greatest amount of time it will generally take for a class of 20 students to complete.

- Table sharing - students remain seated at their tables and share their pictures with their table-mates. Depending on how many are seated at one table, this can take just a couple of minutes.
- Teacher sharing - collect all the papers and go through them one by one, acknowledging each child's drawing and handing it to him/her to put away after you've showed it to the class. This takes less than five minutes, but is generally less fun for the students.
- Pair students with their Kindness Pals to share their pictures with each other and then put them away. This takes less than five minutes once the pals are matched up.
- Sitting in a circle, ask each student to put their papers on the floor in front of them and place their hands in their laps. Start with one student and move in order around the circle. When it's someone's turn to share they pick up their paper, hold it facing outwards so the group can see it, tell about it, and then go put it away (folder, backpack, cubby, and so on) and come back to the group. This takes approximately 5-10 minutes for a group of 20 students.
- Popcorn sharing - call on a student to "pop" up to the front of the class, share the picture, call on another student to pop up, then "pop" over to their backpack/cubby to put their picture away and return to their seat. It takes approx. 10-15 minutes for this sharing "game" for a class of about 20 students. Students love this one but it does take a bit more time.

NOTE: *Try to avoid having just a few students share their drawings and not everyone. If one shares, generally everyone will want to at this young age. They are all proud of their work!*

Give students about five minutes or so to work on their thought bubble drawings. Those who finish quickly can draw another thought on the back of their paper. Then give the quiet signal.

Have each child talk share, using one of the strategies listed above. Here we will use the Kindness Pal time to share pictures with new pals.

Kindness Pals

Say: *Today we're switching Kindness Pals, so let's share our pictures with our new pals! Today we'll hold our bubbles above our heads, the way thoughts look in books and cartoons.*

Hold up your own drawing above your head as a model. ***"I feel happy when I think about_____."***

Say: *Listen carefully for your name, and remember to say "Okay!" and smile at your new pal. Once all the names are called out, you may go find your pal and show your happy thought pictures to him or her. What is a kind thing you could say about your pal's picture?* (I like your drawing, good coloring, nice work, and so on.)

Call out new Pals, adjust for any absences, and when all are matched up give the children a few minutes to share. Remind pals to try to find something kind to say about their partner's drawing. When time is up, have students give a friendly goodbye to each other before returning to their seats.

Closing: *This week try to notice any particular thoughts in your thought bubbles, and we'll tell about them next time. See you then!*

Optional Lesson Extension:

Book – *What is A Thought? (A Thought is A Lot!)* by Amy Kahofer and Jack Pransky. Read this book with the class to further explore thoughts and how they shape our lives.

Comics – Bring in age-appropriate comic books or newspaper comic strips. Have children find and cut out examples of thought bubbles and speech bubbles. See if they can notice any relationship between the character's thoughts and feelings.

Week 10
Others Have Thoughts and Feelings, Too

OBJECTIVES: Review the concept of "thought bubbles" and apply to the thoughts and related feelings of others.

> ASCA Standards:

B-SS 4. Demonstrate empathy

PREPARE: Bell or chime

Opening: *Hello class! Did anyone have any thoughts since we last met? Of course you did! Scientists have proven that we have thousands and thousands of thoughts <u>every single day</u>, isn't that amazing?*

Call on several students who want to share a thought. You might need to encourage students to keep their thoughts short to allow time for others to share.

 Mindfulness Practice

Say: *Because we have so many thoughts zooming around in our brains, it can be hard to focus on just one thing at a time. If we could see everyone's thought bubbles they would all be filled with different pictures right now.* (Use the thought examples just shared.) *Max is thinking about recess, and Carla is thinking about her dog, and everyone has their own different thoughts going on inside their own thought bubbles.*

Say: *During our Mindful Moment today we are going to try to notice whatever thoughts we are having in our thought bubbles. Pay attention to what's going on in your thoughts. Are you thinking about your breathing? Are you thinking about sounds you hear in the class when it's very quiet? Are you thinking about something that happened earlier today? Are you thinking about something you want to do later today? Are you thinking about something imaginary? All of these are <u>thoughts</u>, and all of them are perfectly fine to be having.*

*Now it's time for us to get in our mindful bodies, close or cover our eyes, and take three deep belly breaths. Smell your flower…blow the petals….****Repeat twice more****.*

Notice what's happening right now. You may notice sounds inside the classroom, your breathing, or something else. We will tell what we noticed in a few moments after I ring the bell and we raise our hands. For now, we will continue to be quiet and just notice all that is happening right now.

After a period of quiet, ring the bell, raise your hand when it stops, and open your eyes.

Ask: *Who would like to share a thought you noticed in your thought bubble right now?*

Call on all students who raise their hands and give affirmations to all who share.

 Lesson

Say: *Remember last week when we each drew a happy thought in our thought bubbles? Were our pictures all the same or all different?* [Some were the same and some were different] *Why do you think some were different?*

Discuss how each person has their own thoughts and feelings, and these may be different than our own. What makes YOU feel very happy when you think about it may not be the same thing that makes someone else feel very happy to think about.

> TEACHING TIP: For students with social learning differences this may be a difficult concept that requires some individual work. Enlist the help of the school counselor or other helper if needed. This is an important skill for all children to develop, though for some it will take more time than is allotted here.

Say: *As we've learned, we all have many different feelings. When Paco thought about getting a shot, how did he feel?* [Worried/Scared] *Many of you said you also feel the same way Paco does. But does everyone feel that same way?*

Usually there will be one or two kids who say they do not mind getting a shot. If that isn't the case, use yourself as an example or make up a different one.

Say: *When I think about getting a shot, I <u>do not</u> feel worried or scared. I feel glad and comforted because I think about how a shot protects me from getting sick, and it's actually a good thing for my body. Try to think about that for just a moment. Imagine my thought bubble over my head* (make the gesture of a bubble over your head with your hands) *and inside is me getting a shot. My feeling in my body is _____?* (rub your hand over your heart as they recall your glad feeling.)

Discuss how everyone has their own thought bubbles, and just like you can imagine your own thoughts inside a thought bubble, you can try to imagine someone else's thought bubble, too.

Say: *Now we're going to play a little game where I tell you what's in my thought bubble and you try to guess how I'm feeling about that thought. Remember, we can look for clues about how someone feels in their face and body. We can also think about how WE might feel when we think about that thing. It may or may not be the same thing I am feeling. Ready to guess?*

1. Hold your hands above your head to form a bubble and **say:** *My thought bubble is about a big, growling lion* (make a scared face and gestures). *My feeling is* (rub your heart) _____[scared.]

2. Hold your hands above your head to form a bubble and **say:** *My thought bubble is about how just I broke my favorite pencil* (make a frustrated/sad face and gestures). *My feeling is* (rub your heart) _____ [frustrated/sad.]

3. Hold your hands above your head to form a bubble and **say:** *My thought bubble is about a plate of steaming hot lasagna* (make excited/hungry face and gestures). *My feeling is* (rub your heart) _____[excited/hungry.]

Pause to point out that probably not everyone has the same feelings when they think of lasagna. Did everyone feel the same way about the lion and breaking a pencil? Probably not! Reiterate that everyone has their own thoughts and feelings, and these may be very different from our own.

Continue with more examples as time allows, until most students are able to accurately guess the feeling.

 Kindness Pals

Today's pals will sit together and play the thought bubble guessing game described above. Pair up Kindness Pals, making adjustments for any absences. Once everyone is matched up give the following instructions.

Say: *Remember, the first thing we always do is give each other a friendly greeting - high five, handshake, hello, fist bump, "how are you?" or something else.*

Next, one pal will tell what's in your thought bubble (remember to use your bubble over your head) and the other pal will guess what feeling you are having. Then you will switch and the other pal will tell a thought that's in their bubble and you will guess the feeling. Go ahead!

Move about the room to listen briefly to each set of pals. If someone is having difficulty, provide a prompt for that student. For example, suggest he or she think about a familiar part of the school such as the playground, cafeteria, or gym. Feelings about foods are also fairly easy to model for this game as well.

If time permits, invite pals to share whether this was easy or hard for them. Of course, no one can know everything someone else is thinking, but if we remember that everyone has thoughts and feelings, we can usually make good guesses about what they are.

Closing: *This week try to notice any thoughts or feelings you think someone else might be having, and we'll tell about them next time. See you then!*

Optional Lesson Extensions:

Morning Meeting – Teachers can incorporate thought bubbles into their morning meetings and in talking about the daily agenda. Using an actual thought bubble with the desired topic drawn in can be particularly helpful for those times when everyone needs to be focused on the same thing at the same time.

Thoughts and Feelings Drawings – After students have looked at comic books or other examples of thought bubbles in writing, give each a simple stick figure character to embellish with events that cause a particular feeling. For example, tell the class the character is feeling scared and have them draw the thought to show why the character is scared.

During Conflicts – Thought bubbles and feelings can help students work out simple misunderstandings. When a situation arises, encourage the children involved to try to name the other person's thought and feeling, and then have each child state their own thoughts and feelings.

Unit 3
Mindful of Others

Mindfulness Skills – Heartfulness and Gratitude

Target quiet time during mindfulness ≅ 40 seconds

Week 11
Heartfulness and Kindness

OBJECTIVES: Use the practice of heartfulness to send kind thoughts to someone else; practice kindness and tolerance for differences with a group activity.

> ASCA Standard:

B-SS 4. Demonstrate empathy

PREPARE: Bell or chime

TEACHING TIPS: Starting in this lesson and moving on, the children will be asked to think or say things in their minds but not out loud. Depending on the maturity of the group, this may be something to practice before hand. You can do this by stating a simple phrase and asking everyone to repeat it silently. Whispering or mouthing the words is okay, too, and will be easier for some children to do than keeping completely silent. Remember, the important thing is that they are engaged in the activity, not that they are completely silent during it. If the group repeats the phrases aloud together, that is okay too.

Opening: *Hello class! Did anyone notice another person's thoughts and feelings that were different than yours? Remember, we all have our own thoughts and feelings that are often different from each other.*

Call on several students who want to share what they noticed about thoughts and feelings.

Mindfulness Practice

Say: *Today we are going to begin practicing something called* <u>heartfulness</u> *during our Mindful Moment. We will be doing that by thinking about a person we love very much. It may be your mom or dad, your teacher, or your kindness pal from last week. Each person's bubble will be different, but we will all try to think about a special person.*

Encourage everyone to picture a loved one inside their thought bubbles, but not to say the person's name out loud. During the Mindful Moment, everyone will think about a special person they love, then share who that person was afterwards.

Instruct the class to get in their mindful bodies, close their eyes, and take three deep breaths together.

Say: *And now, we're going to look at that person we love in our thought bubbles. See if you can see him or her right now. Imagine that person smiling at you.*

Now gently move your hands and put them on your chest near your heart (model it for them), *and we will send some kind thoughts to that person. You can think these words in your thought bubble* [or softly say them aloud] *after me.*

Look at your special person in your thought bubble and think "I care about you," (pause several seconds) *"I hope you are happy,"* (pause again) *"I hope you are healthy,"* (pause again) *"I hope you are peaceful."* (Pause) *"Thank you for all you do for me."*

Last, we will pretend to hug that person tightly, by hugging our own bodies tightly. (Model hugging yourself.) *Now we will continue thinking about our special person for a few more moments, until I ring the bell. If you notice something else in your thoughts, try to gently bring your person back into your thought bubble.*

After a period of quiet, ring the bell, raise a hand, and open your eyes. Invite the children to go around in a circle and share whom they were thinking about during heartfulness if they want to. If they share something else unrelated to today's practice, give a gentle reminder that today we were trying to keep our thoughts on a special person. You can help the student notice that their thoughts were wandering, just like yours do sometimes.

 ## Lesson

Say: *Today during our Mindful Moment we tried to think about another person. For the next several weeks we will continue to practice thinking about other people and treating them kindly, even when we have different thoughts from each other.*

Game: Tell the class you will now play a game to show how students are different from each other. We can still have lots of fun together, even when we notice how we are different.

Instruct everyone stand up and move to one side of the room or the other. Use your arms to point right and left as you call out the following:

Say: *If your hair is curly move to this side, and if it's straight move to that side.* Encourage students to move quickly. *We have different hair. Let's try another one!*

Try some of the following concrete differences until children seem to understand moving quickly from one side of the room to the other based on the criteria.

- Shorts/skirt or long pants
- 4 years old or 5 years old (or 5 and 6 for Kindergarten)
- Sneakers or sandals
- Short sleeves/long sleeves
- And so on

Once children can do this, move into the following preferences or thoughts about what is best.

Say: *Isn't it fun to notice how we are all different? And remember, we each have our own thoughts that might be different from each other, too. Even though we think different thoughts, we can still treat each other with kindness and respect.*

- Pizza or hot dogs
- Cats or dogs
- Summer or winter
- Baseball or soccer
- Reading or counting
- Gym or music
- And so on

Stop frequently during the game to point out how we are all different from one another, and how we have different thoughts about what we like best. Treating each other with kindness means no one is teasing, calling names, or laughing at others for their thoughts or choices.

Especially do this when one side of the room has the majority vote. You might say something like "more people like pizza and only a few like hot dogs. Does it mean that pizza is the best food in the world and hot dogs are not good? Of course not! People have their own thoughts about different things, and that's okay!

> TEACHING TIP: Occasionally during this game, a student's competitive nature pops up and they may start chanting for "their team," as in "Piz-ZA! Piz-ZA!" and followers may take up the chant, too. If this happens, use your quiet signal and pause the game to explain that it's okay to cheer for a team, but during this game we aren't trying to win or lose, and we don't want to make the side with fewer students feel like their

thoughts or ideas aren't important, too. So, no chanting is needed during the differences game!

Say: *Remember, we are all different from each other in many ways. We can see some of our differences with our eyes, but we have many other differences we can't see, like our thoughts and ideas about what is best. We can be kind to each other even when we are very different from one another or think very different things.*

 Kindness Pals

Today Kindness Pals will work together to notice how they are different from each other. Call out Pals, adjust for any absences, and give the following instructions:

1. Sit with your pal in a good listening position.
2. Give each other a friendly greeting.
3. Find out how many ways you are different from each other. Students can use options from the game or they can discuss others.
4. Remind everyone that it's okay to like different things and have different thoughts, and we can still treat each other with kindness. It is NOT okay to say mean words to someone because they have different thoughts or ideas.
5. When time is up give a friendly goodbye to your pal and return to your seats.

Closing: *This week try to practice heartfulness and send kind thoughts to someone else, maybe someone who is very different from you, and we'll tell about your experience next time. See you then!*

Optional Lesson Extensions:

Books - *The Sneetches* by Dr. Seuss, *Everyone Matters* by Pat Thomas, *It's Okay to be Different* by Todd Parr. Choose one of these or the many other great picture books on respecting others to read with the class. Make these books available in your class library.

Drawing – Give students blank paper folded in half. On one side they draw themselves, and on the other they draw their Kindness Pal or a table neighbor. Try to show how many ways they are different from each other in their drawings. If possible, they can add thought bubbles to show what they like that is different from their pal.

We're All On the Same Team

OBJECTIVES: Identify "teamwork" as working together to achieve something you can't do on your own; name the team they each belong to (the class name).

PREPARE: Bell or chime, a large floor-sized puzzle with enough pieces for each student to have one, new Kindness Pal list (See Appendix)

> **ASCA Standard:**

B-SS 2. Create positive and supportive relationships with other students

B-SS 7. Use leadership and teamwork skills effectively in diverse teams

TEACHING TIPS: If kids are still wiggly/talking/touching others during mindfulness, don't panic! It is still very early in the school year, and a lot is being asked of these little bodies all day long. Notice that these are the children who may have more difficulty with self-control and behavioral regulation in general. Mindfulness will be especially beneficial for them, but it will take longer for you both to figure out the best way they can experience it. Consider these students your "special challenge" to work on getting mindfulness to work for them. Some ideas include:

- In a private conversation before or after class, talk with the child. Explain that you notice it's very hard for her to sit still/stay quiet during the Mindful Moment. Tell her that as long as she doesn't disturb others, it is okay to move a little or look around the room.
- Assign the child a special mindfulness spot that is away from touching distance of other students.
- Allow the student to cover, rather than close his eyes. This solves two problems at once; it engages the hands and helps the child stay focused on himself rather than others.
- Give the child a small fidget toy to hold and inspect quietly during mindfulness.
- Allow movement as long as it is not disturbing others nearby.
- Remember, a key component of mindfulness is non-judgment. There is no way to "do it wrong," even for wiggly kids.

Opening: *Hello class! Did anyone practice heartfulness for another person during the week? It can be hard to "train your thought bubbles" to think about another person for a few moments, but the more we practice the better we all will get!*

Call on several students who want to share their experiences with heartfulness.

 Mindfulness Practice

Say: *Today we are going to practice <u>heartfulness</u> again during our Mindful Moment. Remember, we are also practicing training our thought bubbles on just one thing. Today we will be doing that by thinking about a person we love very much. It may be your mom or dad, your teacher, or your kindness pal from last week!*

Encourage everyone to picture a loved one inside their thought bubbles, but not to say the person's name out loud. During the Mindful Moment everyone will think about a special person they love, then share who that person was afterwards.

Instruct the class to get in their mindful bodies, close their eyes, and take three deep breaths together.

Say: *And now, we're going to look at that person we love in our thought bubbles. See if you can see him or her right now. Imagine that person smiling at you.*

Now gently move your hands and put them on your chest near your heart (model it for them), *and we will send some more kind thoughts to that person. You can think these words in your mind* [or say them aloud softly] *after me. Look at your special person in your thought bubble and think "I care about you,"* (pause several seconds) *"I hope you are happy,"* (pause again) *"I hope you are healthy,"* (pause again) *"I hope you are peaceful."* Pause. *"Thank you for all you do for me."*

Last, we will pretend to hug that person tightly, by hugging our own bodies tightly. (Model hugging yourself.) *Now we will continue thinking about our special person for a few more moments until I ring the bell. If you notice something else in your thoughts, try to gently bring your person back into your thought bubble.*

After a period of quiet, ring the bell, raise a hand, and open eyes. Invite the children to go around in a circle and share whom they were thinking about during heartfulness. If they share something else unrelated to today's practice, give a gentle reminder that today we were trying to keep our thoughts on a special person. You can help the student notice that their thoughts were wandering, just like yours do sometimes.

 Lesson

Say: *Last time we talked about ways we are different, and today we will be talking about some ways we are the same. Make a T with your hands* [like a time-out signal, with one palm flat across the tips of your other hand's fingers] *if you've ever been on a team.*

Take responses: soccer team, baseball team, and so on.

Say: *When we are on a team, we don't do things by ourselves. We help each other so that we can get more done than we would be able to do on our own, like scoring home runs in baseball, or cleaning up a big mess, or building a cool block tower. That's called* <u>teamwork!</u>

Give the following simple definition of teamwork: *Teamwork means working together with other people to try to get something done.*

Tell the class that everyone can make a T with their hands to show they are part of a team, because everyone in the class is on a team. **Ask** if anyone can guess the name of their team.

Say: *It's the (Teacher's name) Team! And everyone in your grade is on the ___ team. And everyone in this school is on the _____ team! We are all on the same teams!*

Encourage students to think of other ways everyone in the class is the same. Examples include two eyes, ten fingers, bodies, hands, being human, and so on.

Say: *Just like with your sports and other types of teams, you will all work together to do many fun activities this year that you wouldn't be able to do by yourselves. In fact, we're going to do a fun activity right now and we will use* <u>teamwork</u> *to get it done easily!*

Bring out the floor puzzle and explain that is a big puzzle with a lot of pieces, and it takes a long time for one person to put it together alone. One person might not be able to put it together by the time class is over. But since we are working as a team, we can all work together to put the puzzle together quickly.

Say: *Would the _____ Team like to help me put my puzzle together right now? Great, let's get started!*

Ask the class to sit in a circle for this activity. Hopefully by now there is an established routine for doing so. Once the class is sitting in a large circle, give the following instructions:

Each child will get one piece of the puzzle, look at it and then hug it close to the chest. This prevents children from fiddling with it, and also from looking at each other's pieces and trying to fit them together.

The "team puzzle spot" will be in the center of the circle, so everyone needs to watch that spot to notice when they need to place their piece of the puzzle.

When a student notices that their piece matches something in the puzzle spot, they raise their puzzle piece high into the air so it can be seen.

Pass out the pieces. After everyone has a piece, take one of the leftover pieces and place it in the center. If there are none left over, select a child to put a piece down first. Describe the colors and images on the piece, and ask who sees something similar on their own piece. When children raise their puzzle piece, let them come to the center one at a time to see if it fits. Allow them to try several spots before giving assistance, as puzzle skills can vary widely at this age. The puzzle will be quickly put together in this manner.

When it is complete, step back and have everyone admire their teamwork in getting the beautiful puzzle together quickly and easily. After a moment to admire the puzzle, thank everyone for their teamwork, explain that you will put it away while they chat with their Kindness Pals.

> TEACHING TIP: Young children naturally want to help the teacher clean up in all aspects, but doing so in a group setting like this can be distracting to the lesson overall, and/or cause unintended problems such as hurt feelings over who gets to help or snatching pieces from others. How to clean up as a team is a learned skill that takes more time than is allotted here. It could make for an interesting lesson extension, though!

 Kindness Pals

Today everyone will get a new Kindness Pal. Pals will tell about different teams they are on and how their teams work together. Encourage kids to think about their families and other groups they belong to as a "team." Pals can also talk about ways they are the same.

Call out new Pals, adjust for any absences, and give the following instructions:

1. Sit with your pal in the listening position we've practiced: legs crossed, knees almost touching, shoulders pointing at each other.
2. Give each other several friendly greetings.
3. Name the teams you belong to, including your class team and family team.
4. Tell what you do on that team and how you work together to get big jobs done.
5. Try to find five ways you and your pal are the same.
6. Give a friendly goodbye to your pal and return to your seats.

Closing: *This week try to notice how you work together with your teammates to get a big job done quickly, and we'll tell about it next time. See you then!*

Optional Lesson Extensions:

Book - *Swimmy* by Leo Lionni. Read this book to the class, pointing out how Swimmy and his friends used teamwork to swim together and chase the big fish away, something they were unable to do at the beginning of the story when each fish was swimming whichever way it wanted to.

Art Activity – Use blank puzzle piece templates (widely available for free online) for each child to color/draw on. Then label each piece with the child's name in bold marker, and fit the pieces together as a class project. Hang in the room as a reminder that each student is a part of the class team.

Week 13
Sharing and Taking Turns

OBJECTIVES: Apply previously-learned skill of heartfulness to oneself; define and practice sharing and taking turns.

PREPARE: Bell or chime, and

- An interesting item that can be passed around easily such as a small stuffed animal (not a ball or anything hard)
- 10-15 small items in a concealed box or bag - enough to give one to each Kindness Pal pair (colored paper clip, rocks, math manipulatives, and so on)

> ASCA Standards:

B-SS 6. Use effective collaboration skills to work effectively in diverse teams

B-SS 7. Use leadership and teamwork skills effectively in diverse teams

TEACHING TIP: Most classes will have established routines for sitting in rows on the carpet to listen to a story and for sitting in a circle on the carpet for demonstration lessons. If your class has not yet done this, work with them outside of *Peace of Mind* class to help get these two important routines established. Not only will it be helpful for *Peace of Mind* class, it will help the class run more smoothly all the time!

Opening: *Hello class! Have you been using teamwork to help you do awesome things since I saw you last? If you did, I'd like to hear about it!*

Call on several students who want to share their experiences with teamwork.

 Mindfulness Practice

Say: *Today we are going to practice <u>heartfulness</u> again during our Mindful Moment. Remember, we are also training ourselves to think about just one thing. Today we will be doing that by thinking about a <u>really special person</u> we love very much. Today we are each going to think about and send kind thoughts to ourselves!*

Encourage everyone to picture themselves inside their thought bubbles. During the Mindful Moment everyone will think about themselves and what makes them special.

Instruct the class to get in their mindful bodies, close their eyes, and take three deep breaths together.

Say: *And now, we're going to look at ourselves in our thought bubbles. See if you can see yourself right now. If it's really too hard to do, look down at your lap or your legs.*

*Now gently move your hands and put them on your chest near your heart (*model it for them*), and we will send some kind thoughts to ourselves. You can think these words in your mind [*or softly say them aloud*] after me. "I care about me," (*pause several seconds*) "I hope I am happy," (*pause again*) "I hope I am healthy," (*pause again*) "I hope I am peaceful." (*Pause*) "I love you." Last, we will hug ourselves tightly. Now we will continue thinking about ourselves for a few more moments until I ring the bell. If you notice something else in your thoughts, try to gently bring your thoughts back to your very special self.*

After a period of quiet ring the bell, raise hands, and open eyes. Invite the children to tell how it felt to practice heartfulness for yourself. If they share something else unrelated to today's practice, give a gentle reminder that today we were trying to keep our thoughts on heartfulness for ourselves.

> TEACHING TIP: Sending kind thoughts to oneself may be difficult for some children, such as those with learning differences and/or an under-developed sense of self. You may want to prepare that child for the activity ahead of time, or enlist the help of someone else (counselor, social worker) to help you do so. It may help for the child to hold a small picture of himself and speak to the picture. It's perfectly fine for a child to continue to send heartfulness to someone else, too, if that is easier.

 Lesson

Say: *Last week we learned that we are all on the same team in this class. That means we help each other out. If someone needs something we have, we <u>share</u> it. We also <u>take turns</u> when we're on a team since everyone can't do everything at the same time. Remember when we made our puzzle using teamwork? We had to take turns putting our pieces down since we couldn't all put in our pieces at the same time.*

Explain that sharing and taking turns help us work together better as a team. We are being kind when we share our belongings with others, and we are thinking of others' feelings when we allow them to have a turn at something.

Tell the class you have something special to show them, and bring out your interesting object. Ask who would like to hold the item. Everyone will raise their hands.

Say: *Hmm, I have a problem here. I'd like everyone to get a turn, but we can't all hold this at the same time. How can we each get a chance to hold this and look at it?* Let the children tell you they can share it and take turns holding it.

Say: *Great idea! We will share this and take turns passing it to one another. But what will happen if one person takes a loooong time looking at it before passing it on?* (We might run out of time for everyone to get to hold it.) *So to make sure everyone on our team gets a chance to hold this, we must each take just a moment to look/feel/hold it, then pass it on to your teammate next to you.*

Ask students what they think might be in each other's thought bubble now (holding the item and then passing it on to the next student).

Remind students to think about others' feelings if they are tempted to keep the item a little longer, and encourage them to remind themselves that they need to be quick or someone else might not get a turn. It may be helpful to have students count softly: 1-2-3-pass.

Have the students sit in a circle and pass the item around the room, praising and encouraging everyone who passes the item quickly. As time allows, pass the item around again as a reward for everyone working together so well. Point out how we can all have more fun when we work together, share, and take turns. Put the item away and prepare for working with Kindness Pals.

Say: *I have some more items to share with you today. After you greet your pal, I'll come around and give you and your pal one item out of my bag to look at. After you've had a moment to look at it, pass it to your pal. You may have enough time to pass it back and forth several times until our time is up. Remember, if you hold the item too long your pal may not get a chance to look at it, and how will he or she feel?*

Kindness Pals

Call out Kindness Pals, adjust for any absences, and give the following instructions:

1. Sit with your pal in the listening position we've practiced: legs crossed, knees almost touching, shoulders pointing at each other.

2. Give each other several friendly greetings.

3. Take turns sharing the object you are given, passing it back and forth several times. You can also try both holding the object and looking at it together.

4. Switch objects with partner pairs so that each pair gets to hold and share 3 or more different objects.

5. Give a friendly goodbye to your pal and return to your seats.

> TEACHING TIP: Encourage students to notice their partners' thoughts and feelings during this activity to be sure both partners have fun!

Collect the objects as students move back to their seats.

Closing: *This week try to notice how sharing makes others feel good. Send yourself some kind thoughts, too. We'll tell about heartfulness and sharing next time. See you then!*

Optional Lesson Extensions:

Books to extend Heartfulness for oneself: *I Like Myself!* by Karen Beaumont and *I'm Gonna Like Me: Letting Off a Little Self-Esteem* by Jamie Lee Curtis. Read these books to the class and encourage each child to name one or more traits about themselves they really like.

Book to extend sharing concepts: *Should I Share My Ice Cream?* By Mo Willems and *Share and Take Turns* by Cheri J. Meiners. Read these books to the class to reinforce concepts of sharing taught in **Peace of Mind** class.

Week 14
Needs and Wants

OBJECTIVES: Apply feelings of gratitude; contrast needs with wants and tell three of each.

PREPARE: Bell or chime, *optional* pictures of needs and wants (see suggestions below)

> ASCA Standards:

B-SS 9. Demonstrate social maturity and behaviors appropriate to the situation and environment

B-SS 3. Create relationships with adults that support success

Opening: *Hello class! Have you been sharing and taking turns since I saw you last? Did you practice heartfulness for yourself or someone else?*

Call on several students who want to share their experiences.

 Mindfulness Practice

Say: *Today we are going to practice a type of <u>heartfulness</u> called <u>gratitude</u> during our Mindful Moment. Gratitude means a feeling of thankfulness. We can feel thankful for many things and people in our lives. Who would like to name something or someone you feel very thankful for?*

Provide simple examples such as the classroom, teacher, school, parent, or home they live in.

> TEACHING TIP: For very young children it can be difficult to come up with an idea during open-ended assignments. Try giving one concrete idea for the whole class, and encourage students to think of something else if they're inclined to do so. That way everyone has an idea and those who are developmentally ready to branch out on their own may do so.

Say: *Today, let's all try to think about how lucky we are to have such a wonderful school to attend every day. If you want to think about something else you feel grateful for, that's okay too.*

Instruct the class to get in their mindful bodies, close their eyes, and take three deep breaths together.

Say: *Now gently move your hands and put them on your chest near your heart* (model it for them), *and we will send some thankful thoughts to our school and* *the people in it. You can think these words in your mind after me. "My school is a good place,"* (pause several seconds) *"my school has people who help me,"* (pause again) *"I feel thankful to be a part of this school." Now we will continue thinking about our school and how lucky we are to be here for a few more moments, until I ring the bell. If you notice something else in your thoughts, try to gently bring your thoughts back to feeling thankful for your school and the people in it.*

After a period of quiet, ring the bell, raise one hand, and open eyes. Invite the children to share how it felt to practice thankfulness, or gratitude, for the school (or whatever else was chosen). If they share something else unrelated to today's practice, give a gentle reminder that today we were trying to keep our thoughts on feeling thankful. You can help the student notice that their thoughts were wandering, just like yours do sometimes.

 Lesson

Say: *Today we are going to talk about things we need, and how that is different from things we want. Many times we get confused about which is which (grown-ups too!), and we think we NEED things when we really just WANT them. Today we will learn how to tell the difference.*

Introduce the idea that needs are something we can't live without, and wants are everything else. Show pictures of various items and have kids sort them into needs and wants, or just talk about the following and have children name to which category each item belongs.

Needs	Wants
Food	Candy
Water	Soda/other drinks
Air	Toys
Shelter/housing	Cars/bikes
Clothing	Extra clothing
Medicine	Electronics
Love	Pets

Discuss why each need is something vital to living, while each want is not. Wants can be very fun and interesting to have, but they aren't necessary in order to live.

Say: *It's important to remember the difference between needs and wants, because not everyone in our world is fortunate enough to have everything they need. If you do have everything you need, it's important to remember to be thankful for that!*

|

If appropriate, discuss the concept of donating items to others in need:
Sometimes if families have extras, they give some things away to others who need them. This might be extra clothes you don't fit in anymore, extra toys you don't play with, or extra food your family is able to give. This is called "donating" and is a very kind and helpful thing to do if you are able to. Be sure to talk with a parent before deciding to donate any of your things you don't need, and they can help you decide the best way to do it.

Conclude the discussion by reminding students to remember to use the words "want" and "need" accurately from now on, and to remember to give thanks when we have what we need.

Kindness Pals

Call out the Kindness Pal partners and adjust for any absences. This is the last week they will have the same pal, so remind them to be extra kind and thankful for their pal today. Give the following instructions:

1. Sit with your pal in the listening position we've practiced: legs crossed, knees almost touching, shoulders pointing at each other).

2. Give each other several friendly greetings.

3. Tell your pal three things you have that you NEED in order to live.

4. Each pal completes the statement "I'm thankful for_____."

5. Give each other a friendly goodbye and return to your seats.

Closing: *This week try to notice the needs you have in your life, and remember to feel grateful, or thankful, for having them. We'll share what we noticed next time. See you then!*

Optional Lesson Extensions:

Book/Class Book – *The Thankful Book* by Todd Parr. Read this to the class, and create a class Thankful book with each student's drawing of what he or she is thankful for. Keep this class-created book in the library for reading throughout the year.

Art/Drawing – Continuing the theme of gratitude for the school, have a discussion about all the staff who work together in the school (teamwork!) to help make it a nice place. If staff pictures are available, show these to the students and talk about the jobs they may not always see. This could include cafeteria workers, custodians, security guards, aides, front office staff, and so on. Label blank sheets of paper with various staff names and distribute these to students to make a personalized Thank You card for all their hard work in making the school a clean, safe, and fun place. If possible, allow students to deliver these cards personally to the staff person.

Week 15
What Is A Compliment?

OBJECTIVES: Choose a person for whom one feels grateful; practice giving a compliment; notice how receiving a compliment makes one feel.

PREPARE: Bell or chime, puppet, Kindness Pals List (See Appendix)

> ASCA Standards:

B-SS 2. Create positive and supportive relationships with other students

B-SS 3. Create relationships with adults that support success

TEACHING TIPS: Teach students the "me too" signal to use when they have something in common with a character in a story or the puppet. Extend the thumb and pinkie fingers while keeping the other fingers folded, and point your thumb at your chest and then outward. This simple gesture helps children express their similarities without disrupting or calling out.

Opening: *Hello class! Did you notice any feelings of gratitude, or thankfulness, since I saw you last? Who or what made you feel thankful this week, and did you let someone know how you feel?*

Call on several students who want to share their experiences with gratitude.

Mindfulness Practice

Say: *Today we are going to practice <u>gratitude</u> again during our Mindful Moment. Remember, gratitude means a feeling of thankfulness. Last week we thought about how thankful we are for our school. Today we are going to try thinking about a special person, such as a parent, grandparent, or other close family member we are very thankful to have in our lives. This may be the same person you thought about when we practiced heartfulness. Does everyone have a special person in mind? Okay, let's get ready to send some gratitude towards that person!*

Instruct the class to get in their mindful bodies, close their eyes, and take three deep breaths together.

Say: *Now gently move your hands and put them on your chest near your heart (model it for them), and we will send some thankful thoughts to our special person. You can think these words in your mind after me. "Thank you for your love*

and care," (pause several seconds) *"thank you for all you do for me,"* (pause again) *"I am grateful to have you in my life."* Now we will continue thinking about our special person for a few more moments, until I ring the bell. If you notice something else in your thoughts, try to gently bring your thoughts back to your special person.

After a period of quiet, ring the bell, raise a hand, and open eyes. Invite the children to share how it felt to practice thankfulness, or gratitude, for their person or whatever else was chosen. If they share something else unrelated to today's practice, give a gentle reminder that today we were trying to keep our thoughts on feeling thankful. You can help the student notice that their thoughts were wandering, just like yours do sometimes.

Invite students to share whom they were thinking about and to whom they sent thoughts of gratitude, if they are inclined to do so.

 Lesson

Say: *To go along with our gratitude practice, today we're going to learn about how to give and receive <u>compliments</u>. Does anyone know what that word means? Let's get our pal Paco to help us!*

Call on students who want to give ideas on the meaning of compliments. Then bring out Paco, who is excited to see everyone since he hasn't visited the classes in several weeks.

Say: *Hi Paco! Today we're talking about giving and receiving compliments. Would you like me to give you a compliment?*

Puppet: *Oh, yummy yummy! Isn't that a fancy word for ketchup and mustard? You know I love to eat ketchup with my fries!*

Say: *Umm, Paco I think you're talking about a con-di-ment, not a com-pli-ment! Condiments are something we add to our foods, like ketchup and mustard, but that is different than a compliment.*

Puppet: *So, I can't eat it? But you said you're going to give it to me!*

Say: *Yes, we do give compliments to other people. Compliments are the nice words you say to someone when you notice something about that person that you like. It's really easy and fun to do, and doesn't cost any money.*

Puppet: *Ohhhh, now I'm starting to understand! But not really. Where can I find a compliment to give to someone?*

Say: *Well, you have to first notice something you like about someone, and then think about the words you want to say, then say it like this: Paco, I noticed that you have a very shiny colorful fur coat, and I like it a lot.*

Puppet: *Oh, um, okay, that's nice, um….*

Say: *And when someone gives you a compliment, all you need to say is "thank you."*

Puppet: *Thank you!*

Say: *You're welcome, Paco. How did you feel when I gave you the compliment?*

Puppet: *Well, I got a little warm and felt happy inside.*

Say: *Yes, compliments usually make the other person feel happy, like you just gave them a little present that you can't see or touch. A compliment is a kind of "word gift" that you give to others.*

Puppet: *Now can I try it? I wanted to tell you that I like your _____ today.*

Say: *Wow, thank you very much, Paco! You just gave me a nice word gift, too.*

Puppet: *You're welcome!*

Explain that the basic words for giving a compliment to someone are simply: "I like your _____." Point out that you and Paco exchanged this type of compliment, where you both noticed something about the other person's clothing or appearance that you liked. This is the easiest type of compliment to give. There is also another way to give a compliment that can be a little harder. It goes like this: "I like the way you _____."

Model this with Paco.

Say: *Paco, I'm going to give you another "word gift" or compliment now. I like the way you always get so excited when you see the children.*

Puppet: *Thank you! And I like the way you put me gently away in the bag when I'm done talking to the class!*

Say: *Thank you, Paco. I'm going to put you gently in the bag right now, since we are done talking about compliments.*

Explain that you will spend the rest of the time today giving and receiving compliments with our new Kindness Pals.

Kindness Pals

Call out the new Kindness Pal partners and adjust for any absences. Then give the following instructions:

1. Sit with your pal in the listening position we've practiced: legs crossed, knees almost touching, shoulders pointing at each other.

2. Give each other several friendly greetings.

3. Take turns giving at least two easy compliments to each other using the "I like your _____" format. Remind the receiver of the compliment to say "Thank you" and the giver to say, "You're welcome."

4. Remind them of the deeper compliment: "I like the way you_____" and see if they can give two of these to each other. Remind the receiver of the compliment to say "Thank you" and the giver to say, "You're welcome."

5. Instruct the pals to tell each other how they feel inside after getting such nice "compliment gifts" today.

6. Give each other a friendly goodbye and return to seats.

Call on a few children to share out a compliment they received that made them feel especially good inside.

Closing: *This week try to notice all the nice acts others do for you, and then give a compliment to at least one person. We'll tell about our experiences with gratitude and compliments next time. See you then!*

> TEACHING TIP: **In this curriculum pals will be instructed to give a compliment each time new pals are named, or every three lessons.**

Optional Lesson Extension:

Daily Class Greeting/Closing – Make compliments a part of your class routine. Children can give a compliment to the students at their table, the person in front of them in line. You may also create a class "kindness chain" when seated in a circle during morning meeting, where each student gives the next student a compliment until the circle is completed.

Unit 4
Mindful Senses and My Brain

Mindfulness skills – Sensory Experiences of Hearing, Seeing, Touching, Smelling, and Eating

Target quiet time during mindfulness ≅ 50 seconds

Week 16
Mindful Hearing & Introduction to the Brain

OBJECTIVES: Apply mindfulness skills to hearing sounds; identify three parts of the brain (amygdala, pre-frontal cortex, and hippocampus).

PREPARE: Bell or chime, items to make various noises (see suggestions below), Brainy puppet, Brain diagram (see Appendix)

> **ASCA Standards:**
>
> B-LS 1. Demonstrate critical thinking skills to make informed decisions
>
> B-SS 1. Use effective...listening skills

TEACHING TIPS: Coming back from a break in school is a great time to review expectations and routines for *Peace of Mind* class. Also, the Brainy puppet is neither male nor female; try to use the pronoun "it" to be consistent with children understanding this is representing our brains. About halfway through the program is a useful time to begin using two bells during mindfulness, one to begin the moment and the other to end it. This will help with extending the moment to last a bit longer as well.

TEACHING TIP: Children with heightened sensory awareness and sensory processing disorders (SPD) may need modifications during one or more of these lessons on senses. Because they are already overly sensitive to certain sensations (very frequently touch and sound), bringing awareness to something that is uncomfortable may increase their discomfort. This doesn't mean these children shouldn't participate in the lesson. On the contrary, this type of mindful awareness could help these children very much! Just beware that what some children will label as "soft" and "silky" others may label as "hurting" and "uncomfortable." You may need to work individually with these children, or enlist the assistance of the school counselor or other staff to help you. Talk with the child about the lesson beforehand and figure out an alternate comfortable item the child can touch instead of any that may be unbearable. If the child is eventually able to tolerate touching the item and can label it as uncomfortable, this could be a step towards reducing the reactions to the sensations later on and therefore very helpful for the child ultimately. It is also fine not to do the activity or to continue to feel differently.

Opening: *Hello everyone, did you give or receive any compliments since I saw you last? If you did, I want to know about it!*

*Today we are going to start using our five senses during **Peace of Mind** class. Who can name one of our senses?*

Call on students until all five senses have been named: hearing, seeing, smelling, touching, and tasting.

 Mindfulness Practice

Say: *Today we will be using our sense of <u>hearing</u> during our Mindful Moment. Remember, we learned how to use our whole bodies to hear and listen, not just our ears. Today we will use our whole bodies to listen to some sounds in the room. When you hear a sound, think about what might be making the sound but try not to say it out loud. Just notice it and think it in your thought bubble.*

Model this by making a sound such as tapping the wall or stomping your feet. Model holding your hands above your head to form a circle/thought bubble. Mouth the words "tapping" or "footsteps." Practice with additional sounds as needed.

Review getting in our mindful bodies as sitting up straight and getting as still as possible. You may need to say something like: *"Remember, even if the Mindful Moment is difficult for you, please don't take the moment away from someone else who might be enjoying it."*

Explain that starting today you will ring the bell two times. The first bell will begin the Mindful Moment, and when the sound stops you will all place your hands in your lap and <u>close</u> your eyes, instead of raising a hand in the air and opening your eyes. The second time the bell rings, it will indicate the Mindful Moment is over, and you will raise a hand and open your eyes as usual.

Guide students to get in their mindful bodies and take three deep belly breaths together, and then ring the bell. Model placing your hands in your lap and closing your eyes.

If students raise their hands, quietly let them know they can put them down and continue to listen for other sounds. You might need to remind students to try to keep their eyes closed during this activity, as they will naturally be inclined to look at the sounds they hear.

Make a few different sounds using whatever is nearby. Some ideas include:

- Tapping with a marker or your finger on the board
- Footsteps
- Crinkling paper
- Snapping fingers
- Moving a chair
- Rattling keys

> TEACHING TIP: I have found it best to make sounds the children cannot easily imitate themselves, avoiding sounds such as those you can make with your mouth, as they will be inclined to do so if they can. It just comes naturally; if one child clicks her tongue everyone will soon follow suit!

Allow for a period of quiet after making several of these sounds.

Then ring the bell, raise hands when it stops, and open eyes. Invite children to share a sound they noticed. Name the sounds you intentionally made and allow children to name others they noticed.

Say: *This is what it means to hear or listen <u>mindfully.</u> We notice sounds we probably would not have noticed or paid attention to on a normal day in our regular bodies. It's pretty awesome that you were able to notice so many sounds during our Mindful Moment today! See if you can listen mindfully again sometime on your own.*

 Lesson

Say: *You just noticed lots of sounds by using your ears and your mindful bodies to listen carefully. One of the most important parts of our bodies that helps us with hearing is our brain. Our brains help us to hear and do many other things, too, like breathing. It also keeps our blood flowing and our hearts beating. Our brains are amazing and help us do everything that keeps us alive! Let's look at a picture of our brains.* (Show Brain diagram.)

Explain the three parts in detail, one at a time:

Hippocampus – pickle-shaped area in the middle of our brains that helps us remember things, like what we did on our last birthday, where we put our favorite toys, and our friends' names. Call on a few children to share things they remember, and afterwards tell them that memory is "in" their hippocampus!

Amygdala – ball-shaped area in the middle of our brains, near the hippocampus that helps us with feelings. Call on a few children to name a feeling, and afterwards tell them that feeling is "in" their amygdala!

Pre-Frontal Cortex – front area of the brain behind our foreheads that helps us with choices, making plans, and making decisions like what to eat or what clothes to wear. Explain that this is the last area to develop, and doesn't stop growing until we are adults. Point out that babies do NOT get to make many choices or decisions for themselves, but as we get older we are able to do this. Call on a few children to share their experiences with making choices, or having an older or younger sibling who gets to make more or less choices than they do. That's the work of our pre-frontal cortex, or PFC for short!

Say: *Now let's meet a new friend to help us learn more about our brains. It's a puppet whose name is Brainy!**

TEACHING TIP: To use Brainy, put your hand in the mitten and make a fist, with your thumb folded inside your fingers.

The thumb, inside our fist, is where the **amygdala** is located. The amygdala is our emotional center. All our feelings, big and small, come from our amygdala. Our amygdala also helps us react fast and helps keep us safe from what it believes to be dangerous.

Also inside the fist near amygdala is our **hippocampus** where our memories are stored.

Our fingers that cover the thumb represent our **pre-frontal cortex (PFC)**. The PFC is one of the last parts of our brain to develop. It is still growing and getting stronger each day, and will continue growing until we're adults. The PFC is like our control center and helps us make decisions. It also is the part that helps us calm down when our amygdala has a strong emotion.

Brainy's speech will always be underlined in the script guides.

*Inspired by Dr. Daniel Siegel's hand model of the brain.

Brainy says: *Hello everybody! I am a brain, just like each of you has inside your head. Let me show you some of my special parts that help you each day. Here is the Pre-Frontal Cortex right up front, where I make decisions and plans.* (Use your free hand to point out the zig-zag shape above the eyes representing Brainy's PFC. Brainy's entire face area is actually the PFC area.)

Brainy says: *Here is the Hippocampus, storing my memories.* (Open the palm to show the shape representing the hippocampus, but keep amygdala/the thumb folded flat against your palm. After showing the hippocampus, close Brainy again to speak.)

And before I show you the Amygdala, let me tell you that's the part of the brain that is all emotion, or feelings. You'd still like to see the Amygdala? Okay, here goes!

Flip open Brainy by lifting your fingers up and wave the thumb/Amygdala around, and speak loudly/excitedly.

I'mmmmmmm Amygdala! Heyyyyy everybody, whoooooooo, I feel so excited right now! Hey, how you doing? How you doing? Whoo I gotta get out more, I loooooove to meet new people!

Say: *Hey class, I think Amygdala is excited, what do you think?*

Gradually fold the PFC back down over Amygdala, hiding it inside the puppet once again.

Brainy says: *Well, that was my Amygdala. Guess what? Each of you has your very own amygdala, too! Well, I don't know about you but I'm tired from all the excitement of meeting you today so I'm going to take a rest now. See you again soon though!*

Put Brainy away and show the students how to make the brain model with their hands: Put your hand in the air, tuck your thumb in like you're making the number four, and then close your fingers over your thumb. The four fingers are the PFC, inside the palm is the hippocampus, and the thumb is the amygdala.

Next, tell the students it's time for working with Kindness Pals.

Kindness Pals

Call out the Kindness Pal partners and adjust for any absences. Then give the following instructions:

1. Sit with your pal in the listening position we've practiced: legs crossed, knees almost touching, shoulders pointing at each other.

2. Give each other several friendly greetings - high five, handshake, hello, fist bump, "how are you?" or something else.

3. Use your hand to remember the three parts of Brainy with your partner. See if you can name all three parts and what they do. *You may want to walk around the room with Brainy and model for student pairs.*

4. Invite partners to share out one part and what it does, until all pairs have shared and all three parts of the brain introduced today have been named.

   - PFC = control center, making decisions
   - Hippocampus = memory
   - Amygdala = emotions

5. Give each other a friendly goodbye and return to seats.

Closing: *This week teach someone else about the three parts of our brains using your hand, and you can tell me about it next time. See you then!*

Optional Lesson Extensions/ Mindful Listening Games:

High, Middle, or Low - Use a xylophone, trio chime, or other instrument to distinguish between high, middle, and low sounds. Play each sound and teach students to raise their hands high if they hear a higher note, medium if they hear a medium note, and low if they hear a low note. Then with eyes closed, play one of the sounds while children listen mindfully. After the sound stops they raise their hand up high, in the middle, or down low to indicate which sound they heard.

Same or Different - Play two sounds on the instrument while students close their eyes. If they are the same sound, raise one hand. If they are two different sounds, raise two hands.

Drawing – When seated at tables/desks, give each child a piece of paper to draw sounds they hear. This could include sounds naturally occurring in or out of the classroom, or sounds you add to the environment as in the mindfulness practice.

Mindful Seeing & The Hippocampus

OBJECTIVES: Apply mindfulness skills to seeing; explore the role of the hippocampus in memory.

PREPARE: Bell or chime, Brainy puppet

> ASCA Standards:

B-LS 1. Demonstrate critical thinking skills to make informed decisions

B-SMS 2. Demonstrate self-discipline and self-control

Opening: Say: *Hello class! Did anyone practice mindful listening since I saw you last? Did anyone tell someone else about the three parts of your brain? If you did, I'd love to hear about it!*

Call on students who wish to share, as time allows.

> TEACHING TIP: Sometimes when one child shares something it reminds others of events they want to share, too. This can easily go off topic and take up the majority of your class time. To help avoid that use phrases such as:
>
> • Remember, today we're sharing about ___ or ___. Can you hold on to that thought until after Peace of Mind class is finished and then tell me?
>
> • We have enough time for (number) students to share right now.
>
> • If I don't call on you to share now, I'll try to pick you for sharing later in our lesson.
>
> • I wish we could hear from everyone, but now it's time to move on.
>
> • During today's Kindness Pal time everyone will get to tell your experience, so let's try to wait until then.

 Mindfulness Practice

Say: *Today we are going to continue using our five senses during our Mindful Moment. Last week we used our sense of hearing. What are our other senses?*

Call on students until all five senses have been named: hearing, seeing, smelling, touching, and tasting.

Say: *Today we will be using our sense of seeing during our Mindful Moment. Usually we keep our eyes closed during mindfulness practice, but today we will need to open them when I tell you to so we can see. Even though our eyes are open, we still will not be making any sounds or talking. We will notice what we see and think about it in our thought bubbles.*

Model the first item you will all be noticing with your eyes. Looking at the lines in their palms is a simple way to start.

Ask students to look closely at the patterns in their palms, notice individual lines, colors, marks, and so on.

Colors and shapes are also easy concepts for children to grasp. For example, you might tell the class everyone will be using their eyes to look around the room for the color red. Model this by turning your head all around to look at the room. Explicitly state that you will all stay in your Mindful Bodies position and not be moving about the classroom. When you see something red, look intently at it and mouth the word "red" as you make thought bubble gesture over your head. Invite the students to do it with you, seated and silently. Practice with additional colors and/or shapes as needed.

Remind students that you will ring the bell at the beginning of the Mindful Moment again. That is the time everyone will begin looking for the color or shape you will name. The second time the bell rings it will indicate the Mindful Moment is over and they will raise their hands and bring their eyes back to you.

Guide students to get in their mindful bodies, take three deep belly breaths, and then ring the bell.

Say: *Now let's all practice mindful seeing by looking around the room for _____.* (Choose something different than the colors or shapes you practiced with.) *When you see _____, pause and think it in your brain and then keep looking.*

Wait for a sustained period of quiet time.

Say: *Now we will all look for _____. When you see _____, pause and think about it in your brain and then keep looking.*

Repeat this activity for several target items as time allows. Then ring the bell and raise a hand when it stops. Invite children to share all instances of any of the target items they noticed. Encourage each child to name one item, and assure them that it's okay to name something someone else has already named.

Say: *This is what it means to look or see* <u>*mindfully.*</u> *We notice what we probably would not have noticed or paid attention to on a normal day in our regular bodies. It's pretty awesome that you were able to notice so many [colors/shapes] during our Mindful Moment today! Try to look around the room mindfully again sometime on your own.*

 Lesson

Say: *You saw so many colors just now. How were you able to remember what you saw and tell me about it afterwards? Who knows which part of your body helps you remember? Yes, your brain! Let's get out Brainy to help show us how it works.*

Brainy says: *Hi, everyone! That was great remembering. Does anyone remember which part of me you use to help you remember? It's the hippocampus!*

Open Brainy to show the hippocampus symbol on the palm area. Explain that although this area is quite small it can hold a lot of memories. Use Brainy to explain the following facts:

Memories are events we remember that have already happened. Our hippocampus primarily helps us with *long term memories*, or events that happened a long time ago.

The word hippocampus is Greek for "sea horse" since the shape of our hippocampus is similar to a seahorse or a pickle.

Our hippocampus is located near the center of the brain close to the amygdala.

Our hippocampus continues to grow and store more memories as our bodies grow and get bigger.

If we didn't have our hippocampus, we would have a hard time remembering what happened to us, what we've learned how to do, or how we felt.

Invite children to ask any other questions they have about their brains or hippocampus. If needed, encourage them to look up answers with an adult later at home.

Say: *Wow, Brainy, thank you for teaching us about our hippocampus! Now we just need to remember all those great facts. Hmmm, how can I remember what Brainy just told me? Oh right, I can use my hippocampus to remember!*

Put Brainy away and move on to Kindness Pals.

Kindness Pals

Today's topic will be about mindful seeing and memories. After partnering the students and accounting for any absences, give the following instructions:

1. Sit with your pal in the listening position we've practiced: legs crossed, knees almost touching, shoulders pointing at each other.

2. Give each other several friendly greetings - high five, handshake, hello, fist bump, "how are you?" or something else.

3. Tell each other how many of the target items you found, or anything else you noticed during today's mindful seeing activity.

4. Use your hippocampus to tell about a favorite memory you have, such as a special birthday, a funny event, or even something that happened earlier in the week.

5. Be sure each partner gets a turn to talk while the other one listens. If both pals have talked and KP time is not over yet, tell about another memory.

6. Give each other a friendly goodbye and return to seats.

Closing: *This week try to mindfully notice your favorite colors, then use your hippocampus to remember what you see and tell me about it next time. See you then!*

Optional Lesson Extensions:

Book - *The Fantastic, Elastic Brain* by JoAnn M. Deak. Read this informative book to the class, pointing out the three parts discussed in **Peace of Mind** class: hippocampus, PFC, and amygdala.

Activity – Take the class on a "Mindful Seeing" walk, where children are mindfully looking for a target color or shape as they walk, and noticing it without commenting until the walk is over. This can also be used during class transitions from one classroom to another. As students enter the next classroom, have each name one object they noticed as they walk in the door.

Drawing – When seated at tables/desks, give each child a piece of paper to draw target items they see around the room. For example, "Find three items that are blue," "draw two items you notice that have a circle shape," and so on.

TEACHING TIP: Sometimes books have too much text for small children, especially nonfiction texts. When this is the case, rely on illustrations to explain the text in simple terms, and skip any pages that are too text-heavy. Prior to reading the book you might want to say something like, "this is a very long book so we will not be reading all the words or all the pages. If you notice me skipping some pages, it's so we will have enough time for our other activities today."

Week 18
Mindful Touch & The Overprotective Amygdala

OBJECTIVES: Apply mindfulness skills to the sense of touch; explore the roles of the hippocampus, amygdala and prefrontal cortex in reactions to sensations.

PREPARE: Bell or chime, Brainy puppet, new Kindness Pal list

> ASCA Standards:

B-SMS 2. Demonstrate self-discipline and self-control

B-SMS 7. Demonstrate effective coping skills when faced with a problem

B-SS 2. Create positive and supportive relationships with other students

Opening: *Hello class! Did anyone practice mindful seeing since I saw you last? Can you use your hippocampus now to remember what you did and tell me about it?*

Call on students who wish to share, as time allows.

 Mindfulness Practice

Say: *Today we are going to continue using our five senses during our Mindful Moment. Last week we used our sense of seeing. What are our other senses?*

Call on students until all five senses have been named: hearing, seeing, touching, smelling, and tasting.

Say: *Today we will be using our sense of <u>touch</u> during our Mindful Moment. We will notice some items we touch and think about them in our thought bubbles.*

Model touching your shirt sleeve with one hand. Say aloud that you never really noticed that it feels ___ (soft, comfortable, warm, silky, scratchy, and so on). Continue to think aloud about how this feels on your skin. Invite students to rub their own shirt sleeve and name what they notice about it. Practice with additional items as needed, and be sure children understand they are only touching their own items.

Remind students that you will ring the bell at the beginning of the Mindful Moment again. That is the time everyone will close their eyes and begin paying close attention to the sensations of the clothing or other object you will name. The second time the bell rings it will indicate the Mindful Moment is over, and they will raise their hands and bring their eyes back to you.

Guide students to get in their mindful bodies, take three deep belly breaths, and then ring the bell. When it stops, model closing your eyes and placing your hands in your lap.

Say: *Now let's all practice mindful touch by feeling the carpet [or flooring/chair] we are sitting on. Gently touch it with your fingers. Think about what you notice when you just use your fingers to touch. Is it soft? Is it rough? Does it feel smooth, or wrinkly, or something else?*

Invite students to notice the sensations when they run their fingers over these items. Keeping eyes closed during this activity will heighten awareness of touch.

> TEACHING TIP: Students may be naturally inclined to open their eyes and look at the items you will name, especially since the last mindfulness practice required using their eyes. Encourage them to try "turning off" their seeing today by keeping eyes closed. This will allow the sense of touch to be stronger.

Allow a period of sustained quiet time for mindful touching using the same object, then repeat this activity with a different object as time allows. Direct students to touch several other items of their own clothing or another easily accessible personal object. Some suggestions include:

- their desk (if seated at desks/tables)
- their shoe
- their sock
- their pants leg/skirt
- their hair
- their cheek

Ring the bell, raise your hand when it stops, and open your eyes. Invite children to share their experiences with mindful touching.

Say: *This is what it means to touch or feel something <u>mindfully.</u> We notice sensations we probably would not have noticed or paid attention to on a normal day in our regular bodies. It's pretty awesome that you were able to notice so many different touch sensations during our Mindful Moment today! Try to touch and feel your clothing mindfully again sometime on your own.*

Lesson

Today and for the next two lessons, students will explore the roles of the hippocampus, amygdala, and PFC with regard to senses. For each lesson, use Brainy to model these parts and remind students of their basic functions. A sample script is found below.

Say: *Today we noticed the feeling of items we touched. Our brain helps us notice these sensations. Let's get out Brainy to help show us how.*

Brainy says: *Hi, class! How's everyone doing today? Great! I heard you used your sense of touch to notice how something feels. That reminds me of a time I accidentally touched the hot stove, and* (open palm to wave Amygdala around) *aaaaaaaggh, hot, hot, get away quickly, that's dangerous!* (Close palm to continue telling the story.) *Well, let me tell you, my Amygdala saved me that day because I pulled my hand away so fast I barely got hurt. Whew! And guess what helped me remember that I should never go near the hot stove again? That's right, my good old Hippocampus!* (Open palm to show the hippocampus.) *Those two parts of the brain really help me!*

Explain that the amygdala warns us when we might be in danger and our hippocampus helps us remember that danger. Our PFC helps us think about the sensation and notice whether it is comfortable or uncomfortable. Sometimes our amygdala reacts strongly, but our PFC can help us realize there's not actually danger.

Use Brainy to model this.

Brainy Says: *There was another time my mom bought me new socks. I put them on and wow did they feel scratchy!* (Open palm to wave Amygdala around.) *Aaaaaaaaaggh, take them off, take them off! They're awful, they hurt, I can't wear these!* (Close palm to continue telling the story.) *Oh, Amygdala, calm down. They are just socks, and they are uncomfortable but they won't really hurt you. Take some deep breaths and think about it for a minute. Okay, what can I do? Mom bought me these new socks but I don't like how they feel. Maybe I can tell her they're not comfortable and we can exchange them for some new ones.*

Discuss the above scenarios with students. Emphasize that our amygdala is a great protector, but sometimes it can be a little too protective. This is called our "overprotective Amygdala." Our PFC helps us think about whether or not there is actually danger and make a good decision about how to react. Encourage students to try to think of other times our amygdala might protect us from danger with regards to sensations of touch. Then contrast these with times we might feel uncomfortable but are not in actual danger. In these times our PFC can help us label the sensation as "uncomfortable" and then deal with it calmly.

Use Brainy to model reactions to touching any or all of the following items, using the same basic script as before. At the point where Amydgala starts yelling "dangerous, dangerous, aaaaghh," stop the story and let the students tell whether the situation is actually dangerous or not. Then put Brainy away and move on to Kindness Pals.

Potentially Dangerous	Usually Just Uncomfortable*
Hot items (water, stove, iron, curlers)	Too tight or loose clothes
Sharp objects (knives, scissors, tools)	Chalky/dusty items (flour, chalk, powder)
Insect stings/bites (bees, ants, spiders)	New shoes
	Scratchy/itchy materials (wool, jute)

In certain cases, such as severe allergies, asthma, and so on, these items might also be dangerous.

Conclude by reminding students that sometimes when we touch items (or they touch us) they can be dangerous. Other times, the items are not dangerous but just uncomfortable. Our brains help us think about the best way to respond.

 Kindness Pals

Assign new Kindness Pals today. Today's discussion topic will be about comfortable and uncomfortable sensations. Adjust for any absences, then give the following instructions:

1. Sit with your pal in the listening position we've practiced: legs crossed, knees almost touching, shoulders pointing at each other.

2. Give each other several friendly greetings - high five, handshake, hello, fist bump, "how are you?" or something else.

3. Give your new pal a compliment. Try to use "I like the way you____."

4. Tell about something that feels very comfortable when you touch it (i.e., soft blanket or pet's fur).

5. Tell about something that feels very uncomfortable when you touch it, and how you react. Is it dangerous or just uncomfortable?

6. Be sure each partner gets a turn to talk while the other one listens. If both pals have talked and KP time is not over yet, tell about another comfortable/uncomfortable sensation.

7. Give a friendly goodbye and return to seats.

Closing: *Try to mindfully notice how something feels this week. We'll tell about our experiences next time. See you then!*

Optional Lesson Extension:

Activity: Sensory boxes. Use empty tissue boxes to hold various items and have students guess what they are based on touch alone. You may need to provide blindfolds. Suggestions include: play dough, stones, chalk, pipe cleaners, or other easily recognizable classroom items. Encourage students to describe what they feel ("it's soft and furry" or "it feels dusty and hard") before making a guess about the object.

Drawing: Give each child a piece of paper to draw target items that are smooth, bumpy, soft, and so on. They may need to walk around the classroom to explore and touch various objects, then return to their seats to draw them.

Non-Judgment: Use this and other senses lessons to help children understand and practice the concept of non-judgment. Before labeling anything as good or bad (sights, sounds, smells, sensations, and so on) encourage children to take a moment to think about it first. This valuable concept can also be applied to friends, new encounters, and many more areas.

Week 19
Mindful Smell & More Overprotective Amygdala

OBJECTIVES: Apply mindfulness skills to the sense of smell; explore the roles of the hippocampus, amygdala and prefrontal cortex in reaction to smells.

PREPARE: Bell or chime, items with strong smells (coffee beans, dryer sheet, peppermints, box of crayons, bottle of lotion or perfume, and so on), Brainy puppet

> ASCA Standards:

B-SMS 7. Demonstrate effective coping skills when faced with a problem

B-LS 1. Demonstrate critical-thinking skills to make informed decisions

Opening: *Hello class! Did anyone touch a particularly comfortable or uncomfortable thing since I saw you last? Who remembers which part of your brain helps you stay safe if you touch something dangerous?* (Amygdala)

Call on students who wish to share, as time allows.

 Mindfulness Practice

Say: *Today we are going to continue using our five senses during our Mindful Moment. Last week we used our sense of touch. What are our other senses?*

Call on students until all five senses have been named: hearing, seeing, touching, smelling and tasting.

Say: *Today we will be using our sense of <u>smell</u> during our Mindful Moment. I brought some items for you all to smell. Now, smells are something we usually have strong feelings about. We either really like something or we think it smells terrible. Either way, whether you like this smell or not, I'd like you to try very hard not to say anything and just think about the smell in your thought bubble.*

Take out your first item and show it to the class.

Explain how today's session will work. While they sit quietly with eyes closed or turned downward, you will come around and hold something in front of them to smell. Whether they like the smell or not, they should try to keep the thought in their bubbles and not say it aloud.

For today's mindfulness practice it will work best if students are sitting in a circle. If they are not already in a circle, take the time to move them now.

Remind students that you will ring the bell at the beginning of the Mindful Moment. That is the time everyone will close their eyes and begin paying close attention to the smells you will bring around the room. The second time the bell rings it will indicate the Mindful Moment is over, and they will raise their hands and bring their eyes back to you.

Guide students to get in their mindful bodies, take three deep belly breaths, and then ring the bell. When it stops, model closing your eyes and placing your hands in your lap.

Say: *Now let's continue taking deep breaths and noticing the smell that I bring by.*

Move around the circle of students with each item, pausing briefly in front of each student's nose. After every student has had a chance to smell the item, invite students to think about the smell, what might have been in the bag, and whether they liked the smell or not.

> TEACHING TIP: Students may be naturally inclined to open their eyes and look at the items you bring around. Encourage them to try "turning off" their seeing today by keeping eyes closed. Just like with mindful touch, this will allow the sense of smell to be stronger.

Repeat the above activity with two or three more smells, as time allows.

After a period of quiet time ring the bell, raise hands, and open eyes. Invite children to share their experiences with mindful smelling. You can show them the items you brought around, if they haven't already figured them out.

Say: *This is what it means to smell something <u>mindfully</u>. We notice smells we probably would not have noticed or paid attention to on a normal day in our regular bodies. It's pretty awesome that you were able to notice so many different smells during our Mindful Moment today! Try to smell mindfully again sometime on your own.*

 Lesson

Today and for the next lesson, students will explore the roles of the hippocampus, amygdala, and PFC with regard to senses. For each lesson, use Brainy to model these parts and remind students of their basic functions. A sample script is found below.

Say: *Today we noticed the smells of different items. Our brain helps us notice and react to these smells. Let's get out Brainy to help show us how!*

Brainy says: *Hi, class! Did you use your sense of smell today? That reminds me of a time I was outside and smelled some smoke and* (open palm to wave Amygdala around) *aaaaaaaggh, smoke, fire, get away, go tell someone, that's dangerous!* (Close palm to continue telling the story.) *Well, I ran to get my Grandpa and it turned out to be someone's campfire. But Grandpa said I was right to come and get him because sometimes smoke can be dangerous! Good old Amygdala did its job again! Guess who helps me remember that I should always tell a grownup if I smell smoke? That's right, my Hippocampus!* (Open palm to show the hippocampus.) *Those two parts really look out for me!*

Explain that the amygdala warns us when we might be in danger and our hippocampus helps us remember whether it's dangerous or not. Our PFC helps us think about what we smell and notice whether it is pleasant or unpleasant, or good or bad. Sometimes our amygdala reacts strongly, but our PFC can help us realize whether or not there's actually danger. Use Brainy to model this.

Brainy Says: *There was another time I ran inside the house and smelled something terrible in the kitchen. I went in there and saw broccoli cooking on the stove. I remembered not to go near the stove this time! But that smell, oh…* (Open palm to wave Amygdala around) *Aaaaaaaaaggh, danger, danger, you can't eat that! Oh it's just awful, no way is that going in my mouth!* (Close palm to continue telling the story.) *So my PFC jumps in and says "Oh, Amygdala, it's just broccoli, which is actually healthy for you. It does have a pretty unpleasant smell, but it's not dangerous. Take some deep breaths and think about it for a minute.* (Model Brainy taking deep breaths.) *Okay, what can I do? I can go back outside and get away from the smell right now. Maybe once it's done cooking it will smell better.*

Discuss the following scenarios with students. Emphasize that our amygdala is a great protector, but sometimes it can be a little too protective. This is called our "overprotective Amygdala." Our PFC helps us think about this and make a good decision about how to react. Encourage students to try to think of other times our amygdala might protect us from danger with our sense of smell. Then contrast these with times we might not like a smell, but are not in actual danger. In these times our PFC can help us label the smell as "unpleasant" or "yucky" and then deal with it calmly. Suggestions include:

Potentially Dangerous	Not usually dangerous
Smoke/fire	Broccoli/other food cooking
Cleaning supplies/chemicals	Fishy/seafood market
Food that is too old	Body smells* (sweat, gas, feet)

*TEACHING TIP: Although it may feel uncomfortable for adults, most children will have no aversion to talking about body smells, including bowel movements and passing gas. In fact, they love to talk about these (perhaps a little too much) and they especially love to have big reactions when they notice a body smell. The concept of kind choices will be introduced towards the end of this curriculum, but now is a good time to begin helping children think about how having a huge reaction to someone else's body smell isn't necessary (it's not dangerous!) and also isn't kind.

Use Brainy to model reactions to smelling any or all of the above items, following the same basic script as before. Be sure to model Brainy pausing to reflect on the smell before reacting. Let the students tell Brainy whether something is actually dangerous or not. Then put Brainy away and get ready for Kindness Pals.

Conclude by reminding students that sometimes when we smell items they can be dangerous. Other times, the items are not dangerous but just unpleasant. Our brains help us think about the best way to respond.

 Kindness Pals

Today's discussion topic will be about favorite and least favorite smells. Adjust for any absences, then give the following instructions:

1. Sit with your pal in the listening position we've practiced: legs crossed, knees almost touching, shoulders pointing at each other.

2. Give each other several friendly greetings - high five, handshake, hello, fist bump, "how are you?" or something else.

3. Tell your absolute most favorite smell in the whole world. Tell what it reminds you of, when you get to smell it, and so on.

4. Tell your least favorite smell in the whole world. Tell the last time you smelled it, and how you reacted when you smelled it. Was it a dangerous smell, or just an unpleasant one?

5. Give a friendly goodbye and return to seats.

Closing: *Try to use your sense of smell mindfully, or really pay attention to smells this week. See if you notice a very good smell, or a very bad smell, and how you respond when you smell it. We'll tell about our experiences next time. See you then!*

Optional Lesson Extensions:

Activity – Take the class for a "mindful smelling walk" around the school and spend time noticing the various smells of the cafeteria, playground, gym, and so on. Have students label the smells as *pleasant* or *unpleasant but not dangerous*. If your school has a garden this can be a great activity to do there!

Drawing – When seated at tables/desks, give each child a piece of paper to draw items they smell. This could include smells naturally occurring in the classroom, smells you add to the environment as in the mindfulness practice, or smells the students think fit a certain category, such as pleasant, unpleasant, or dangerous.

Non-Judgment – Use this and other senses lessons to help children understand and practice the concept of non-judgment. Before labeling anything as good or bad (sights, sounds, smells, sensations, and so on) encourage children to take a moment to think about it first. This valuable concept can also be applied to friends, new encounters, and many more areas.

Week 20
Mindful Taste & My Growing Brain

OBJECTIVES: Apply mindfulness skills to the sense of taste and the act of eating; explore the roles of the hippocampus, amygdala, and PFC in taste.

PREPARE: Bell or chime, puppets, one food item for each student. Use school-provided snacks or snacks the students bring from home. If this is not an option, see Teaching Tips below.

> **ASCA Standards:**

B-SMS 7. Demonstrate effective coping skills when faced with a problem

B-LS 1. Demonstrate critical-thinking skills to make informed decisions

TEACHING TIPS: If you will provide the food item, raisins are generally recommended as they are allergy friendly and can be bought in large quantities easily. However, with this young age it is imperative that you also check with teachers/parents beforehand to make sure no one has food restrictions that the child may not be able to or want to articulate.

If there is a child with highly rigid eating behaviors, work with the teacher/counselor/parent to ensure the child has a snack he/she will feel comfortable eating. Do not try to insist the child eat the raisin or other snack you brought, unless he/she expresses interest.

Opening: *Hello class! Did anyone notice a particularly pleasant or unpleasant smell since I saw you last? Did you smell anything that was actually dangerous? How did you react?*

Call on students who wish to share.

Mindfulness Practice

Say: *Today we are going to continue using our five senses during our Mindful Moment. Last week we used our sense of touch. There's only one sense left that we haven't used. Can you guess which one it is?* [Taste]

Say: *Yes, today we will be using our sense of <u>taste</u> during our Mindful Moment. You see, when we eat, we often eat mindlessly, or without really paying attention to our food. Today we are going to eat something in a mindful way, which means we*

are going to pay very close attention to it and notice more details about it than we usually do. Before we eat this food, we're going to use our other senses to explore it, too!

If you are using raisins or another potentially unfamiliar food item you brought:

Tell the class you have brought a small item for each person to taste. Explain that you have checked with the [teachers/parents] and no one is allergic to this food. Even though no one is allergic, some kids may not like this food or may not <u>think</u> they will like it. This could be your amygdala looking out for danger and warning you if something isn't good for you. Assure students that this food is safe and will not harm anyone in any way. In fact, many kids have probably already eaten this food before. At first they will only hold this food item in their hand and follow your directions. When you instruct kids to put it in their mouths, encourage students to use their PFC to mindfully consider this food before they decide they absolutely cannot or won't eat it. <u>No one will be forced to eat the item if they really don't want to!</u> After giving these directions, place a raisin in each student's hand.

If students are eating their own snack from home or a familiar school-provided snack:

Tell the class that today they will eat a small part of their snack during our Mindful Moment. However, instead of eating it the usual way, we are going to be very mindful and take some time to notice details about the snack we may not have noticed before. Everyone is going to try very hard to <u>wait</u> to eat the snack until instructed to do so. First they will only hold a piece of their snack in their hand and follow your directions.

Say: *Okay, now that we all have our food item in our hands we are ready to begin. Everyone please get in your mindful bodies. Let's take three deep breaths together, then I will ring the bell. Remember, we are going to be completely quiet during this time so that we can focus on our food.*

Ring the bell to indicate the beginning of the Mindful Moment. When it stops,

Say: *I'd like everyone to look at the item in your hand. Use your <u>eyes</u> to notice the colors you see. Do you see bumps, or ridges, or another pattern? What else do you notice about your item?* (Pause)

Now use your <u>nose</u> to smell your food. Does it have a pleasant smell? Have you ever noticed this smell before? Breathe it in for a few moments, and think about whether you like the smell or not.

Now use your <u>finger</u> to touch the food item softly. Does it feel smooth? Rough? Bumpy? Or something else? Is it hard or soft? Continue touching the food for a moment more.

Finally we are going to put the [raisin, bite of your snack] on our tongue, but don't chew it yet! Instead, let your mouth close around it. Let it sit on your tongue, inside your closed mouth, for a moment and see what you notice. (Pause)

Breathe in and see if you taste the smell you noticed earlier. (Pause) *Now roll the food around a little on your tongue, and see if you notice the bumps or pattern you saw on it earlier. Can you feel that shape in your mouth?*

Last, move the food over to your teeth and slooooowwwly let your teeth sink into it. Chew it very slowly now, noticing the juice and tastes that squeeze out when you chew. Before you swallow, move your food back over to your tongue one last time. Does it taste different now that you've chewed it some? How is the texture different, do you still notice the bumps or other pattern?

Go ahead and finish chewing your food now, and swallow carefully. See if you can notice the flavor going down your throat, all the way into your stomach. Now we will sit for a few moments more, until I ring the bell, and notice the tastes still in our mouth even though the food is gone.

Give some quiet time for students to notice tastes. If students have their snack, invite them to take another bite in the same way, as time allows.

Then ring the bell and raise your hand when it stops. Invite children to share their experiences with mindful taste and eating. If anyone chose not to eat the raisin, have them throw it away now.

Say: *This is what it means to taste and eat something <u>mindfully.</u> We notice details we probably would not have noticed or paid attention to on a normal day in our regular bodies. It's pretty awesome that you were able to notice so many different things about your food during our Mindful Moment today! We usually eat our food quickly or without really noticing it. Some call that eating <u>mindlessly.</u> Try to eat something mindfully again sometime this week.*

|

Lesson

Say: *Our brain helps us eat mindfully, of course! What do you think our amygdala, PFC, and hippocampus have to do with taste and eating? Let's get out Brainy to help answer that question!*

> TEACHING TIP: Remember that it is perfectly fine to read the puppet scripts directly from this book, as the children's focus will be on your hand with the puppet and not on your face. Just remember to keep moving your hand as you read so the puppet continues to "talk!"

Brainy says: *Hi, everyone! Did I hear someone say eating? That reminds me of the time I ran in the house and smelled that broccoli cooking…wait, did I already tell you that story? I did? Well, let me tell you the rest of it now. I ran outside to play some more, and then when it was time to come in and eat dinner there was the broccoli piled on my plate….* (open palm to wave Amygdala around) *aaaaaaaggh, disgusting, I can't eat that, it's so terrible, it's awful, it's dangerous!* (Close palm to continue telling the story.)

Then, my PFC said "Wait a minute, didn't we just decide broccoli isn't dangerous?" Then my Hippocampus piped up. (Open palm to show the hippocampus, move the thumb/ amygdala out of the way.) *"Yeah, remember broccoli is a vegetable and it's good for you."* (Close palm to continue the story.)

Okay, let me look at this broccoli closely. Hmm, it actually is a nice green color. It has interesting buds on it and looks sort of like a tree. It doesn't have the same smell now, it actually smells kind of good. Maybe I can try a bite, and if I don't like it, then I can calmly ask my mom if I can leave the rest. So that's what I did. And you know what? I actually ended up eating it all, it tasted so yummy!

But if I had just listened to Amygdala I wouldn't have tried it, and dinner might have been a mess. Thanks for looking out for me, Amygdala, but this time it's okay, the broccoli isn't dangerous!

Thank Brainy and put the puppet away. Explain that the amygdala warns us when we might be in danger and our hippocampus helps us remember. Our PFC helps us think, plan, and make a good decision.

Say: *Who has a food they just absolutely hate and never, ever eat?*

Call on a few children to share the foods they do not like. Ask whether or not they tried the food they didn't like, and if they did, how many times have they tried it?

Say: *Sometimes we don't want to try something new, including foods, and we "think" we may not like it even though we haven't tried it, or maybe we tried it once long ago and didn't like it, but haven't tried it in a really long time. Our brains can stretch and grow, though, as we learn to like new foods we didn't use to like at all.*

If you used the raisin or another unfamiliar snack, discuss here how kids felt about it initially. If someone was hesitant to eat the raisin but did so in the end, invite the child to tell about it. If someone chose not to eat the raisin, that's okay too. Invite that child to tell about it.

Explain that sometimes we have to "teach" our amygdala that something is actually safe. We do this by using our PFC to stay calm, try the food, and think it over. Once our amygdala realizes there is no danger, we don't have that same reaction the next time we try the food. This is one of the ways our brain is always stretching and growing, and learning new information. (Of course, sometimes there might really be danger, like when we have a food allergy or food is spoiled, and our amygdala is doing its job in keeping us safe.)

 Kindness Pals

Today pals will work together to think about foods they used to not like, but over time have learned to like and now eat regularly. They can also tell about foods they still don't like to eat, and think about whether Amygdala is warning of real danger. Remind them that just as our bodies grow and change, our tastes change too, and we might need to try something a few times before Amygdala realizes there is no danger in it.

Call out pals, adjust for any absences, then give the following instructions:

1. Sit with your pal in the listening position we've practiced: legs crossed, knees almost touching, shoulders pointing at each other.
2. Give each other several friendly greetings - high five, handshake, hello, fist bump, "how are you?" or something else.
3. Tell about a food you used to refuse to eat, but now have learned to like.
4. Tell about a food you still do not like, and whether or not there is any danger in eating it.
5. If yes, choose to continue listening to Amygdala and stay away from that food. If not, can you make a mindful choice to try it again?
6. Give a friendly goodbye and return to seats.

Closing: *Try to use your sense of taste mindfully, really paying attention to how foods taste this week. We'll tell about our experiences next time. See you then!*

Optional Lesson Extensions:

Book - *I Will Never Not Ever Eat a Tomato* by Lauren Child. Read this book with the class (or watch it via YouTube or SchoolTube) and discuss Lola's reaction to the foods her brother tries to get her to eat for lunch. Although we can't see inside Lola's brain in the pictures, what was her amygdala doing? Her PFC? Her hippocampus? How did mindfulness help her eat the foods?

Drawing – When seated at tables give each child a blank paper with a circle on it. Ask them to draw a new food or two they will try or try again. Remind them to examine the food mindfully, as we did with the raisin/snack, before tasting it. Involve parents in this activity if possible and encourage them to send in pictures (via text, email, and so on) of students trying their chosen foods at home. Emphasize that it is perfectly fine to not like the food and to decide not to eat it anymore, but it is important to try new foods!

Non-Judgment – Use this and other senses lessons to help children understand and practice the concept of non-judgment. Before labeling anything as good or bad (sights, sounds, smells, sensations, and so on) encourage children to take a moment to think about it first. This valuable concept can also be applied to friends, new encounters, and many more areas.

Unit 5
Mindful Self-Calming

Mindfulness Skills –Body Scan & Muscle Relaxation

Target quiet time during mindfulness ≅ 60 seconds

Week 21
Mindful or Mindless?

OBJECTIVES: Scan bodies to notice feelings; synthesize previous lessons on using our brains to categorize behaviors as "mindful" or "mindless."

PREPARE: Bell or chime, new Kindness Pal list

> ASCA Standards:

B-SS 2. Create positive and supportive relationships with other students

B-SS 5. Demonstrate ethical decision-making and social responsibility

B-LS 1. Demonstrate critical-thinking skills to make informed decisions

Opening: *Hello wonderful wunderkinds! Did anyone eat something <u>mindfully</u> since I saw you last? Did you try a new food and help your brain stretch a little bit?*

Call on students who wish to share, and restate the definitions for <u>mindful</u> and <u>mindless</u>:

Mindfully = paying close attention to what you're doing

Mindlessly = doing something without noticing it or paying much attention to it

Mindfulness Practice

Say: *Today we are going to spend our Mindful Moment paying very close attention to our bodies. I will call out a part of our body and we will all try to think about that part and notice how it is feeling. Then we'll move on to the next part. We call this a "Body Scan" because we will focus for a moment on each part of our whole bodies. Are you ready to try this with me? Great!*

Invite students to get in their mindful bodies and take three deep belly breaths together. Ring the bell to indicate the beginning of the Mindful Moment. When it stops, model closing your eyes and placing your hands in your lap.

Say: *I'd like everyone to notice your <u>feet</u>. Wiggle your toes a little bit. How does that feel? Notice if your feet feel comfortable, hot, cold, sore, or something else.* (Pause)

Next, move on to your <u>legs</u>. They are probably bent into a crisscross shape. Notice how strong they are, and how flexible they are to bend like that. Pay attention to your legs for a moment. (Pause)

Next, notice your <u>stomach and chest.</u> This area is also called your <u>torso</u>. Is it feeling good? Does it feel tight, or stuffy, or something else? Think about your stomach and chest for a moment and notice how they are feeling right now. Do you feel your heart beating? (Pause)

Now let's move on to our <u>shoulders and arms</u>. Move them around a little and notice how that feels. Is there any tightness? Gently roll your shoulders a bit and notice if that feels better. How are your arms? They carry a lot for you every day. Pay attention to how they feel right now while they are resting. (Pause)

Last, let's notice our <u>head</u>. How does your head feel? It is heavy or light? Do you notice anything hurting, or does it feel good? Pay attention to how your head feels for a moment. Move it around a little if you want to, and notice how that feels. (Pause)

After a period of quiet, ring the bell and raise your hand when it stops.

Invite the children to share what they noticed about their bodies during the body scan activity.

Say: *That was our first body scan practice. When we really pay attention to each part of our bodies, we notice all sorts of feelings we didn't realize were there before. How do you think paying attention to our bodies like that can help us?* [Notice injuries, be able to tell someone exactly where something hurts, appreciating our bodies and how they work, noticing where feelings are stored in our bodies, and so on.]

 Lesson

Say: *Today we are going to talk more about the words "mindful" and "mindless." We know that mindful eating means we are paying close attention to the taste and everything about our food, while mindless eating is when we eat quickly without really noticing how foods taste.*

Help students think back to the previous lessons on mindful hearing, seeing, touching, and smelling. When we paid close attention, we noticed lots of sounds, colors, textures, and smells we might have otherwise missed out on. Discuss the opposite of each term and what it might be like to do something mindlessly.

Mindful Action	Opposite	Possible Outcome
Mindful hearing	Mindless hearing	Not noticing sounds in nature; not really hearing what someone is saying to us; missing directions
Mindful seeing	Mindless seeing	Not noticing beautiful colors or other sights; not seeing something we are looking for even when it's right in front of us
Mindful touching	Mindless touching	Not noticing sensations/ feelings; touching dangerous items by accident
Mindful smelling	Mindless smelling	Not noticing smells around us, good or bad
Mindful tasting	Mindless tasting	Not noticing how delicious some foods taste; over-eating; eating something that might not be good for you; not stretching your brain to learn to like new foods

Say: *Which way do you think we use our senses most of the time, mindfully or mindlessly?* [mindlessly] *Yes, most of the time many of us rush through our day without paying much attention to the beautiful sights, sounds, smells, and sensations around us. Which way can help us feel peaceful and happy? Of course, mindfully! Can we choose to use our senses mindfully if we want to? Yes, and we have been using our mindful senses for the last several weeks!*

When we think about other actions we do at school like walking, speaking, and playing do we also have choices to be mindful or mindless? Discuss the following behaviors. Use Brainy and/or Paco to act out the "possible outcomes" if desired.

Mindful Action	Opposite	Possible Outcome*
Mindful walking around the classroom	Mindless walking	Bumping into furniture, stepping on kids, crashing into each other
Mindful talking/speaking to each other	Mindless speaking	Talking at the same time, shouting, saying words that aren't kind
Mindful playing	Mindless playing	Accidentally breaking someone's toy, knocking over a block tower, messing up a puzzle

Conclude that mindful walking, talking, playing, and other actions all involve <u>paying more attention</u> and <u>being more careful</u> than mindless actions. In most cases, we can definitely choose to be mindful with our actions. Choosing mindful actions almost always leads to more fun for everyone!

*Of course, these possible outcomes could also be intentional acts and therefore "mindful," without being kind. These scenarios presume that children generally have positive intentions. The subsequent lesson on Choosing Kind addresses this issue in more detail.

 Kindness Pals

Assign new Kindness Pals today. Today's topic will be about mindful and mindless actions. After partnering the students up and accounting for any absences, instruct them to do the following:

1. Sit with your pal in the listening position we've practiced: legs crossed, knees almost touching, shoulders pointing at each other.

2. Give your new pal several friendly greetings, followed by a compliment.

3. Tell about a time you did something in the classroom mindlessly, without noticing what you were doing, such as crashing into someone, accidentally knocking over something, and so on.

4. Tell about a time you did something mindfully, paying close attention to what you were doing, such as artwork, creating something with blocks, writing, and so on. If students can't think of a time, they can talk about one of their mindful senses experiences.

5. Be sure each partner gets a turn to talk while the other one listens. If both pals have talked and KP time is not over yet, tell another example of mindless and mindful actions.

6. Give a friendly goodbye and return to seats.

Closing: *Try to notice when you are doing something mindfully or mindlessly, with or without really paying much attention, this week. We'll tell about our experiences next time. See you then!*

Optional Lesson Extensions:

Video – *Furry Potter* by Sesame Street. In this Harry Potter parody, Cookie Monster has to listen carefully to the directions in order to get to the cookies. Pause the video to ask children to consider whether Cookie's actions are <u>mindful</u> or <u>mindless</u> as he attempts to enter the castle.

Drawing – Give students a blank paper and instruct them to illustrate a mindful action on one side and a mindless action on the other side. They can use some of the examples shared in class, such as walking, speaking, or playing, or come up with their own action.

Week 22
Choosing Kind

OBJECTIVES: Relate "making a choice" to intentional actions, and practice using this intention to make mindful and kind choices with others.

PREPARE: Bell or chime, puppets

> ASCA Standards:

B-SS 4. Demonstrate empathy

B-SS 9. Demonstrate social maturity and behaviors appropriate to the situation and environment

Opening: *Hello again! Did anyone do something <u>mindfully</u> since I saw you last? Or did you notice yourself doing something <u>mindlessly</u>? I'd love to hear about either experience!*

Call on students who wish to share, and restate the definitions for <u>mindful</u> and <u>mindless</u> as needed:

Mindfully = paying close attention to what you're doing

Mindlessly = doing something without thinking about it

 Mindfulness Practice

Say: *Last week during our Mindful Moment we noticed our bodies by doing a Body Scan. Today we are going to try that again. I will call out a part of our body and we will all try to think about that part and notice how it is feeling. Then we'll move on to the next part. We call this a "Body Scan" because we will focus for a moment on each part of our whole bodies. Are you ready to try this with me again today?*

Invite students to get in their mindful bodies and take three deep belly breaths together. Ring the bell to indicate the beginning of the Mindful Moment. When it stops, close your eyes and model placing your hands in your lap.

Say: *I'd like everyone to notice your <u>feet</u>. Wiggle your toes a little bit. How does that feel? Notice if your feet feel comfortable, hot, cold, sore, or something else. (Pause)*

Next, move on to your <u>legs</u>. They are probably bent into a crisscross shape. Notice how strong they are, and how flexible they are to bend like that. Pay attention to your legs for a moment. (Pause)

Next, notice your <u>stomach and chest.</u> *This area is also called your* <u>torso</u>. *Is it feeling good? Does it feel tight, or stuffy, or something else? Think about your stomach and chest for a moment and notice how they are feeling right now. Do you feel your heart beating?* (Pause)

Now let's move on to our <u>shoulders and arms</u>. *Move them around a little and notice how that feels. Is there any tightness? Gently roll your shoulders a bit and notice if that feels better. How are your arms? They carry a lot for you every day. Pay attention to how they feel right now while they are resting.* (Pause)

Last, let's notice our <u>head</u>. *How does your head feel? It is heavy or light? Do you notice anything hurting, or does it feel good? Pay attention to how your head feels for a moment. Move it around a little if you want to, and notice how that feels.* (Pause)

Ring the bell. Students raise hands and open eyes when it stops. Invite the children to share what they noticed about their bodies during the body scan activity.

Say: *When we really pay attention to each part of our bodies, we notice all sorts of feelings we may not have realized were there before. When we notice any places in our bodies that aren't feeling so good, we can do something about it to help our bodies feel better!*

 Lesson

Say: *Today we are learning about making a* <u>choice.</u> *What does the word* <u>choice</u> *mean?*

Call on students to share their ideas. Conclude that choice means having the power to choose between two or more options; being able to pick something you want.

Say: *Who remembers which part of our brain helps us make choices?* [Our pre-frontal cortex, or PFC] *Sometimes adults make choices for you to help keep you safe and healthy, like choosing your bedtime or choosing when it's time for you to visit the doctor. However, there are still plenty of times where you DO have the power to choose something for yourself. Let's think of those times now.*

Call on students to share times they have the power to make a choice. You might hear or suggest:

- Choosing food in a grocery store or restaurant
- Bringing an item for snack/lunch
- Which clothes to wear (sometimes parents don't give you a choice if it's not safe for the weather)
- Which toy to play with
- Attending centers (often called "Choice Time")
- Playing a game at recess
- Friends to play with at recess

Explain that as you get older, your PFC grows and gets stronger and you have more power in making choices. When you have this power, you can also choose to be kind or unkind in your responses to others. When we are being mindful of our words, actions, and the feelings of others, we will also be making kind choices. Sometimes we say words mindlessly, or without paying much attention to our words, and we may also be unkind.

Say: *We are going to figure out whether some choices are mindful and kind, or mindless and therefore possibly unkind. We will have our puppets help us model some choices.*

Use Paco and Brainy to act out the following scenarios together. Have them take turns making kind and unkind/mindless choices.

> TEACHING TIP: If you have been using a puppet as indicated up to now, you are likely feeling more confident and can tackle having a puppet on each hand. This means you are voicing three different characters: your own as the teacher and those of your two puppets. If it feels too confusing to use both Paco and Brainy at the same time, you can take on the role of one character yourself and talk back and forth with just one of the puppets, using the examples that follow.

Choosing kind with nicknames:

Puppet Says: *Hi Brainy-Brainy-Bo Bainy! How are you today?*

Brainy: *Um, Paco, I don't really like it when you say my name like that, and I'd like you to stop.*

Puppet: Huh, *but I wasn't teasing, it wasn't mean, you're my friend so why can't I call you that if I want to? Brainy-Brainy Bo Bainy! Brainy-Brainy Bo Bainy!*

Discuss whether or not Paco is being mindful of Brainy's feelings. He has a choice to make: continue saying the words Brainy didn't like, or choose to stop, or use other words. Which is the kind choice? Redo the scene using some suggestions from the students.

Puppet says: *Hi Brainy-Brainy-Bo Bainy! How are you today?*

Brainy: *Um, I don't really like it when you say my name like that, and I'd like you to stop.*

Puppet: Oh, gee Brainy I didn't realize you didn't like it, I'm sorry. How about this: Hi Brainy my friend, how are you today?

Emphasize that this time Paco is making a kind choice because he is being mindful of Brainy's feelings. Even though he might have liked saying Brainy's name that way, Brainy did not like it so the kind choice is to stop saying it.

Choosing kind with words:

Puppet says: *Hey Brainy, look at this picture I just drew. Do you like it?*

Brainy examines the pretend picture: THAT? No way! It's the worst drawing I ever saw!

Puppet (looks down and speaks in a sad voice): Oh.

Discuss whether or not Brainy is being mindful of Paco's feelings with the words used here. How can Brainy be both honest about not liking the drawing but still be mindful of not hurting Paco's feelings? [Avoid words like "worst," tell another drawing that Paco did like, suggest they draw a picture together, and so on.]

Puppet: *Hey Brainy, look at this picture I just drew. Do you like it?*

Brainy examines the pretend picture and thinks aloud: *Hmm, I don't really like that picture but want to be mindful of Paco's feelings.* (Now he speaks loudly to Paco) *Well, it's not my favorite one, but remember that train you drew the other day? I really liked that one!*

Choosing kind with actions:

> **Brainy says:** *Oh, I'm so excited to go to the Lego Center today, I've been wanting to play Legos all day!*
>
> **Puppet: Oh, me too, I want to go the Lego Center too. What's that? There's only one space left, the teacher said, and it's my turn to choose next. I'm choosing the Lego Center!**

Discuss whether or not Paco is being mindful of Brainy's feelings. He has a choice to make: take the last spot in the Lego Center, or give it to Brainy because Brainy has been talking about it all day. Which is the kind choice? Discuss how Brainy can be mindful of Paco's feelings, too, and offer to make sure Paco gets to go to the Lego Center next time.

Model how both puppets can make kind choices here:

> **Brainy says:** *Oh, I'm so excited to go to the Lego Center today, I've been wanting to play Legos all day!*
>
> **Puppet: Oh, me too, I want to go the Lego Center too. What's that? There's only one space left, the teacher said, and it's my turn to choose next. Well, I know you really love the Lego Center, Brainy, and have been wanting to go all day, so I'll choose another Center and you can have the last spot at Legos.**
>
> **Brainy:** *Oh, thank you Paco! I'll give my space to you next time.*

Discuss and model other scenarios of choosing kind as time allows. Examples may include:

- Choosing kind to let someone else go first during a game (explored further in Week 25)
- Choosing kind when lining up
- Choosing kind at the water fountain

 Kindness Pals

Today's topic will be about the power of choice and choosing to be kind. After partnering the students up and accounting for any absences, instruct them to do the following:

1. Sit with your pal in the listening position we've practiced: legs crossed, knees almost touching, shoulders pointing at each other.

2. Exchange friendly greetings.

3. Tell about a time you made a kind choice, perhaps giving up what you wanted and allowing someone else to get what they wanted instead.

4. Be sure each partner gets a turn to talk while the other one listens. If both pals have talked and KP time is not over yet, tell about another choice you made.

5. If students can't think of an example to discuss, have them act out one of the scenarios from today's lesson. One student plays the part of each puppet, and then they can reverse roles so each gets a chance to choose kind.

6. Give a friendly goodbye and return to seats.

Closing: *Choose to be kind to others this week whenever you can, and we'll tell about our kind choices next time. See you then!*

Optional Lesson Extensions:

More Bucket Filling – *Have You Filled A Bucket Today?* by Carol McCloud. There are many books in this series, and accompanying activities galore on Carol's website: www.bucketfillers101.com. There is also a catchy song and video called Fill Your Bucket by The Learning Station. Incorporating these activities into your classroom or as a unit will help children practice making kind choices throughout their day, week, month, and the rest of the school year.

Kindness Journals – Give students a blank journal (or blank pages stapled together) to draw or write about one kind act they did for others or others did for them each day. Try to keep it up for a whole week, or incorporate this into your weekly writing center topics. Research shows that documenting kind acts increases the likelihood of more kind acts in the future!

Kindness Jar – Keep track of class acts of kindness by filling a jar with marbles or colored glass stones for each kind act reported or observed. In the midst of a lesson, try to spot kindness and comment on it: "I just noticed Dillon pick up Keyara's pencil when she dropped it, so I'm adding another marble to our jar!" and then continue with the lesson. When the jar is filled the whole class earns a special activity or reward. Even if children initially are clearly doing kind acts to earn the praise and reward, the habit might very well stick around!

Week 23
Calming My Body

OBJECTIVES:	Use body scanning to notice feelings; identify and practice a strategy for calming down.	
PREPARE:	Bell or chime, puppets, feelings thermometer from Week 8 (See Appendix)	

> ASCA Standards:

B-SMS 7. Demonstrate effective coping skills when faced with a problem

B-SMS 10. Demonstrate the ability to manage transitions and ability to adapt to changing situations and responsibilities

Opening: *Hello lovely learners! Did you make kind choices since I saw you last? I'm quite sure you did, and I'd like to hear about it!*

Call on all who want to share an experience of choosing to be kind.

Mindfulness Practice

Say: *We are going learn something we can do with our bodies when we notice a big feeling, or feel stress somewhere in our bodies. This strategy is called "muscle relaxation." We're going to relax our muscles by following some simple instructions. We will need to squeeze our bodies, and then let go. When I say "squeeze your body" it means to tighten up all your muscles.*

Model closing your fists, bringing your arms in close to your body, and "squeezing" your muscles up tight while inhaling deeply. Then let go and release your arms and fists with a soft sigh. Have students practice once or twice so they know what to do.

Instruct students to get in their mindful bodies and take three deep breaths together. Ring the bell to indicate the start of the Mindful Moment, and model closing your eyes while placing your hands in your lap.

After the sound stops, say: *Now we'll smell our flowers as we squeeze in (pause), and blow our petals as we let go. (Pause) Breathe in and squeeze…..and breathe out and release…..Let's try it one more time. Breathe in and squeeze…..and breathe out and release. Now see what you notice about how your body feels. I'll be quiet so we can focus on our bodies right now for a few moments.*

After a period of sustained quiet, ring the bell again. After hands raise and eyes open, invite students to share what they noticed about their bodies after the muscle relaxation exercise.

Call on all who want to share something they noticed about their bodies and muscle relaxation, as time allows.

 Lesson

Bring out the feelings thermometer from Week 8. Review each level and what it means:

1 = Calm, cool, relaxed

2 = A small feeling is noticed, like a shoe bothering you, or needing water, and so on.

3 = A feeling is getting bigger or heating up, and is starting to bother you more.

4 = A feeling is getting hotter, taking up your whole body, and you may start crying.

5 = A feeling becomes too big for your body and explodes out. This usually looks like a tantrum or meltdown of some sort.

Review the term "calm down" as presented in Week 8: moving from a higher number to a lower number on the feelings thermometer. Remind students of the story about Paco getting shots and going to a 5. Tell the class that today we will use Brainy to retell the story and show what might happen inside our brains when we have a big feeling.

Say: *Brainy, you have a story about a number 5 feeling, and I'd like you to tell it to the class.*

Brainy says*: Oh, you mean that time I had to get a...you know what? Okay, here's what happened. I was at home watching my favorite cartoons. I was at a 1, feeling cool and calm. Then, my mom said "Brainy, we have to go to the doctor's office today." I thought, hmm, why are we going to the doctor today? I'm not sick! I was a little worried. My feelings were at a 2. Mommy, why do I have to go to the doctor? I'm not getting a shot, am I? Just the thought of having to get a shot put me up to a 3! I HATE shots! And you know what she said? "Yes, Brainy, you have to get a shot today." Ohhhh no! Now my feeling was a 4.* **Begin opening the fingers to "flip Brainy's lid."**

I started whimpering and crying a little. Please no, Mommy, I don't want to get a shot today! But we had to get in the car and drive to the doctor's office. I resisted going in, but my mom pulled me inside. I sat and cried until it was time to go in the exam room. The doctor got out the needle, came over to me, and that's when it happened. I went to a 5! **Fully flip open your fingers and have Amygdala wave around, screaming *"Noooooo!"***

Say: *If Brainy had been able to do a mindful body scan to notice any feelings, do you think it might have helped? Which part of our brain helps us remember things like what a mindful body scan is?* [the hippocampus] *What else could Brainy try to do to bring the big feelings back down to a smaller number?* [belly breathing, or something else]

Re-enact the scene above one last time, only this time Brainy will use the hippocampus to remember to do a body scan and take some deep breaths when it notices tightness and worry in its body. Then, the PFC will make a plan and choose which actions to take.

Say: *Brainy, let's try that one more time. This time show the class how your hippo-campus can help you remember to scan your body, notice feelings getting bigger, and then do something about it before your amygdala takes over, and how your PFC helps you choose what to do next.*

Brainy Says: *OK, here's what happened. I was at home watching my favorite cartoons. I was at a 1, feeling cool and calm. Then, my mom said, "Brainy, we have to go to the doctor's office today." I thought, hmm, why are we going to the doctor today? I'm not sick! I was a little worried. My feelings were at a 2. Mommy, why do I have to go to the doctor? I'm not getting a shot, am I? Just the thought of having to get a shot put me up to a 3! I HATE shots! And you know what she said? "Yes, Brainy, you have to get a shot today." Ohhhh no! Now my feeling was a 4.* **Begin opening the fingers to "flip Brainy's lid."**

Then my hippocampus kicked in and reminded me of some strategies I've learned to do when I start getting big feelings. **Open palm to show the hippocampus, but keep Amygdala tucked down flat or slightly wiggling but not upright.**

I'm getting some big feelings. I can scan my body to notice where the feelings are. My feet feel like running. My legs do too. My tummy is hurting. My chest feels tight. My hands want to hide my face. I have to do something! What can I do to calm my body down? Oh, I remember, I can take some deep belly breaths, too! PFC, what's the best choice here? I can use some strategies to calm down, or start screaming and fall on the floor.

Begin to close Brainy slowly as you model belly breaths. *Okay, let's choose to do some calming strategies. Smell my flower, blow my petals. Smell my flower, blow my petals. Now I notice my feet feel a little more still. Smell my flower, blow my* *petals. My tummy is not hurting as much. Smell my flower, blow my petals. My face doesn't need to hide, it will be okay.*

Mommy, I don't like to get shots, but I know they're important. Let's get this over with quickly!

Tell how Brainy was able to continue taking deep breaths and stayed calm until the shot was over. Remind students that shots don't really hurt as much as we think they do!

Ask children to share some times they had a big feeling recently.

Use Brainy to re-enact a few of the children's scenarios, both with a mindless reaction and a mindful one. By now, hopefully you are adept at using the puppet and can create your own dialogue. Here are some possible examples of **flipping your lid**:

> **Stopping a preferred activity:** *Oh, I'm having fun watching TV! I love this show. What's that, Dad? You said I have to turn it off right now? But… but…* (Amygdala pops out) *I don't wanna! It's not fair! My show isn't done! Waaaaaahhhh!*

> **Breaking something:** *I love this Lego creation I just built! It's so awesome. Huh? It just broke apart when I picked it up! Ohhhhh……* (Amygdala pops out) *Nooooooo! I worked so hard on it, now it's in pieces everywhere! I'll never get to build it again, aaahhhhh!*

Here are some examples of taking a **Mindful Moment** and self-calming:

> **Stopping a preferred activity**: *Oh, I'm having fun watching TV! I love this show. What's that, Dad? You said I have to turn it off right now? But…but…* **Open palm to show hippocampus, keeping amygdala folded down** *I remember my body scan. I'm feeling angry in my chest. I can take some deep breaths and see if it helps. What should we choose to do, PFC?* **Model three belly breaths and the PFC slowly coming back into place**. *Okay, Dad, I was hoping to finish this show but I can turn it off now because it's getting late.*

> **Breaking something**: *I love this Lego creation I just built! It's so awesome. Huh? It just broke apart when I picked it up! Ohhhhh……* **Amygdala pops out** *Wait! I notice my hands are in fists, ready to break apart the rest of this Lego. I remember that this happened before and I got even angrier when I broke it all to pieces. That might not be the best choice I can take. Take deep*

breaths, I can try to rebuild it. **Model three belly breaths and the PFC slowly coming back into place.**

Explain that in order to calm down we can use strategies to help us. Remind the students that a "strategy" is something we can do that helps us. We need to use our hippocampus to remember the strategies that will help us calm down when we notice we are getting a big feeling, like anger. Then our PFC helps us make a plan and choose what to do next. Body scanning and belly breaths are two strategies that can help us calm down.

 Kindness Pals

Today Kindness Pals will work together to tell about a time they had a big, 5-sized feeling **and how they calmed down afterwards**. After everyone is paired up and any absences are accounted for, give the following instructions:

1. Sit with your pal in the listening position we've practiced: legs crossed, knees almost touching, shoulders pointing at each other.
2. Exchange friendly greetings.
3. Tell each other about a time you had a really big feeling.
4. Pretend to be having that feeling again, but this time try doing a quick body scan followed by belly breathing and then choose a more mindful response.
5. Ask everyone to show how much they think doing a body scan followed by belly breathing helps them calm down using thumbs up, down, or in the middle.
6. Give your pal a friendly goodbye and return to the circle.

Closing: *Try to notice how your body is feeling when you start to have a big feeling, and try to do something about it right away! We'll tell about our experiences next time. See you then!*

Optional Lesson Extensions:

Book – *Waiting Is Not Easy!* by Mo Willems. Read this book to the class and pause to discuss what is happening in Elephant's brain as he gets impatient waiting for Piggie's surprise. What could he do to stay calm while waiting? Ask the students to name times they become impatient waiting, and how they can think through the best options and make a different plan.

Video – *Star S'Mores* by Sesame Street. In this adorable video, Cookie Monster must use self-control to calm down and resist eating the cookie. Show this to students and pause the video to discuss what might be happening in Cookie's brain each time he tries to eat the cookie. Use Brainy to help model Cookie "flipping his lid" and grabbing the cookie, then remembering a strategy and using it to try to control himself. See if students can model Cookie's three strategies after the video: count to four, sing a song, and imagine the cookie is something else.

|

Week 24
More Ways to Calm Down

Objectives: Review and practice previously learned strategies for self-calming; name and practice at least three additional strategies to help oneself calm down.

Prepare: Bell or chime, new Kindness Pal list

> ASCA Standards:

B-SS 2. Create positive and supportive relationships with other students

B-SMS 7. Demonstrate effective coping skills when faced with a problem

B-SMS 10. Demonstrate the ability to manage transitions and ability to adapt to changing situations and responsibilities

Opening: *Hello everyone! Did anyone try muscle relaxation or another strategy to calm your body down this week? I'd like to hear about what happened and how you handled it.*

Call on all who want to share about calming down, as time allows.

Mindfulness Practice

Say: *We've been learning about strategies to help us calm down. Today we're going to practice our strategy of muscle relaxation again. Remember, we're going to relax our muscles by following some simple instructions. We will need to squeeze our bodies, and then let go. When I say "squeeze your body" it means to tighten up all your muscles.*

Model closing your fists, bringing your arms in close to your body, and "squeezing" your muscles up tight while inhaling deeply. Then let go with a soft sigh. Have students practice once or twice so they know what to do.

Instruct students to get in their mindful bodies and take three deep breaths. Ring the bell to indicate the start of the Mindful Moment. After the sound stops, model closing your eyes and placing your hands in your lap.

Say: *Now we'll smell our flowers as we squeeze in* (pause), *and blow our petals as we let go.* (pause) *Breathe in and squeeze…..and breathe out and release…..Let's try it one more time. Breathe in and squeeze…..and breathe out and release….and now see what you notice about how your body feels. I'll be quiet so we can focus on our bodies right now for a few moments.*

After a sustained period of quiet, ring the bell again. After students raise a hand and open their eyes, invite them to share what they noticed about their bodies after the muscle relaxation exercise.

 Lesson

Explain that having big feelings is not bad, and we all get them sometimes. However, we must be sure not to hurt ourselves, others, or objects when we have these feelings. It is important to do something about the feelings. If the first strategy we try doesn't work, we need to try another one. It's important to know many different ways we can try to help ourselves calm down.

Discuss the fact that there are many strategies to help us calm down, and we've already learned about four in the past few weeks. Ask students to name and explain any of the strategies you've learned in class so far. They include:

- Belly breathing
- Body scan
- Muscle relaxation

Say: *Great job remembering our strategies! Your hippocampus is helping you out! Let's practice these together right now. And remember, your PFC helps you make a plan and choose which strategy or strategies you're going to try.*

Lead students through a brief practice of each strategy named above.

Say: *There are also many other things we do to help ourselves feel better. Who can tell me something that helps you when you're having a big feeling?*

Call on children to share what they usually do when they are angry, sad, mad, and so on, to try to feel better. You are likely to hear:

- Listen to music
- Count to 10
- Go to a bedroom/quiet space
- Punch a pillow
- Drink water
- Watch TV
- Talk to someone
- Color or draw

Model these together with the students, as appropriate. Then pretend to have a big feeling about something (amygdala,) remember some of the strategies (hippocampus,) and choose which action to take (PFC.) Examples include:

- Feeling scared about a thunderstorm or other event
- Feeling angry about having to clean up or stop playing with a toy
- Feeling frustrated while trying to build or create something
- Feeling sad when it's time to say goodbye after a playdate or visit with family

> TEACHING TIP: These can be acted out individually, by calling on a student to come to the front of the class and show what they would do, or as a group with everyone choosing their own strategy and telling about it afterwards. If you choose a few students to act these out, assure the rest of the class they will have a chance to do it with their Kindness Pals in a few minutes.

 Kindness Pals

Assign new Pals today. After accounting for any absences, give the following instructions:

1. Sit with your pal in the listening position we've practiced: legs crossed, knees almost touching, shoulders pointing at each other.
2. Give your new pal several friendly greetings, followed by a compliment.
3. Choose one pal to act out a scenario discussed in class, choose a strategy to calm down, and see if the other pal can guess which strategy was used.
4. Switch roles and have the other pal act out the same or a different scenario while the other guesses which strategy is used to calm down.
5. Tell your pal goodbye and return to the circle.

Closing: *Try to use one of these strategies the next time you're having a problem! We'll tell about how your strategy helped you next time. See you then!*

Optional Lesson Extensions:

Class Book or Poster - Work together to create a class book or poster titled "Ways to Calm Down." Add drawings, icons and simple words to help students remember the strategies named and practiced in class. Keep the poster in the classroom for reference whenever students need to use a strategy to calm down. Place the poster in the library or area children go to when they want to calm down.

Parent Newsletter - Communicate the strategies named during class to parents, and encourage them to help their child to use these at home when needed.

Week 25
Games and Big Feelings

OBJECTIVES: Apply learned concept of *mindful actions* to choosing, playing, and winning or losing games.

PREPARE: Bell or chime, puppets

> ASCA Standards:

B-SS 9. Demonstrate social maturity and behaviors appropriate to the situation and environment

B-SMS 7. Demonstrate effective coping skills when faced with a problem

B-SMS 10. Demonstrate the ability to manage transitions and ability to adapt to changing situations and responsibilities

Opening: *Hello everyone! Did anyone have a problem or a big feeling since we last met? Did you remember to use a strategy like muscle relaxation to help you calm down?*

Call on all who want to share something about using a strategy to calm down.

Mindfulness Practice

Say: *We've been learning about strategies to help us calm down. Today we're going to practice our strategy of muscle relaxation again. Remember, we're going to relax our muscles by following some simple instructions. We will need to squeeze our bodies, and then let go. When I say "squeeze your body" it means to tighten up all your muscles.*

Model closing your fists, bringing your arms in close to your body, and "squeezing" your muscles up tight while inhaling deeply. Then let go with a soft sigh. Have students practice once or twice so they know what to do.

Instruct students to get in their mindful bodies and take three deep breaths. Ring the bell to indicate the start of the Mindful Moment. After the sound stops, model placing your hands in your lap and closing your eyes.

Say: *Now we'll smell our flowers as we squeeze in (pause), and blow our petals as we let go (pause). Breathe in and squeeze…..and breathe out and release…..Let's try it one more time. Breathe in and squeeze…..and breathe out and release….and now see what you notice about how your body feels. I'll be quiet so we can focus on our bodies right now for a few moments.*

After a period of sustained quiet, ring the bell again. After hands raise and eyes open, invite students to share what they noticed about their bodies after the muscle relaxation exercise.

 Lesson

Say: *Today we are going to talk about a time when many kids (and sometimes even grownups) get really upset and forget to make mindful choices. We are going to think about and practice being mindful of our feelings and others when we are* <u>*playing games*</u>*.*

Explain that games such as sports, board games, and recess games like tag are all for one purpose: having fun. When people forget this, their amygdala takes over and they get very focused on winning and losing. They "flip their lids" and forget that games are for having fun. There are also other parts of games people get big feelings about, too, besides just winning and losing.

Use Paco and Brainy to model four scenarios that often occur during a game. Create your own dialogue for the following situations.

> TEACHING TIP: If you have been using a puppet as indicated up to now, you are likely feeling more confident and can tackle having a puppet on each hand AND create your own dialogue as you do so. This means you are voicing three different characters: your own as the teacher and those of your two puppets. If it feels too confusing to use both Paco and Brainy at the same time, you can take on the role of one character yourself and talk back and forth with one puppet, using the examples that follow.

<u>1. Choosing a game</u> -- One wants to play Sweet City (like Candyland) and the other wants to play Hide and Seek.

> **Puppet:** *My favorite game is Hide and Seek, so that's what we're going to play!*
>
> **Brainy:** *No way! MY favorite game is Sweet City, and that's what we're going to play!*

Both insist on their way. If using Brainy, "flip its lid" to show getting angry.

Ask the class: *Are they having fun yet? Do you think they forgot that games are for having fun?* [No, they are not having fun and yes, they forgot that games are all about having fun!]

Then show Paco remembering that games are about fun, so he agrees to play Sweet City since it's a fun game, too and suggests that they can play Hide and Seek later. Brainy agrees.

2. Which color to use -- Once the puppets agree to play Sweet City, they have to decide which color game piece to use. Both want to use the same color, arguing that it's their favorite color so they must have it. In this example, both characters "flip their lids," and start yelling and crying about having to use their preferred color.

> **Puppet:** *I let you choose the game so I should get to choose my favorite color, red!*

> **Brainy:** *But my favorite color is red, too, and I ALWAYS use the red in any game I play!*

Ask the class: *Is it really important to use your favorite color in a game every time you play? Are you more likely to win if you use that color? Is the game more or less fun depending on which color you use?*

Point out that this is not necessarily using our PFC to make the best choice, since the color game piece used really doesn't change the game at all. Take some deep, mindful breaths, and think aloud about how having that color must be really important to the other puppet, and it would be a kind choice to let him have it.

Then have Brainy agree to give the desired color to Paco and choose a different color.

> TEACHING TIP: Anytime the puppets or other characters you create are arguing, be sure to switch the roles so that both characters get to model "flipping their lids" and making a more mindful choice. That way, one character doesn't become the "bad one" while the other is the "good one." In reality, we all flip our lids sometimes!

3. Going first -- Now that the puppets have decided which game to play, and which color each will use, they must decide who will go first in the game.

Ask the puppets: *Who will go first?* Both puppets say ***Me!,*** <u>*Me!*</u> and begin to argue over who will get to go first.

Ask the class: *Are these puppets having any fun yet? Remember, games are for having fun, but Paco and Brainy aren't able to have fun because they are only thinking about what they each want, and not about playing the game and having fun together.*

Ask for suggestions on how children decide who goes first. (Eenie meenie miney moe, hip skip sky blue, and so on)

Say: *Those are all good ways to decide who goes first, but they can take a little time to do. I know a way that's even faster because it only takes two seconds to do. Then you can get started playing a game and having fun more quickly! My way is only <u>two words</u> long: "You can!" That's it.*

Have the children repeat the words "you can." Point out how much shorter that is than the rhymes or other ways of deciding. The longer it takes to decide who goes first, the less time there is for playing and having fun. If the game is played a second time, someone else should go first the next time.

Have Paco or Brainy model saying "You can!" and then the other puppet says "Thank you, next time you can!"

Remind the students that often the person who goes first is NOT the winner, and that going first does not mean you will win.

<u>4. Winning and losing</u> -- Pretend that Paco and Brainy have been playing Sweet City for a while now, and Paco is getting close to the end.

> **Paco says:** ***If I get double purple next time, I'll win. Oh wow, I got double purple!! Yes, I won! I'm the best! Whoo-hoo!*** Brainy flips his lid and Amygdala screams how it didn't want to lose, it hates losing, never wants to play that game again, and so on. Talk with the children about how both puppets are not being mindful of their feelings or each other. Paco is bragging about winning, while Brainy is flipping its lid about losing.

Say: *When we come to the end of a game, whether we win or lose, the kind way to respond is just by saying "Good game!"*

After Brainy calms down (use a strategy!), ask Paco if he wants to play again. Paco says "**No way!**" because Brainy gets too stuck on losing and it's no fun to play. Brainy points out how Paco was bragging about winning and that didn't help him feel better about losing, either.

Remind the puppets to just say "Good game." Re-do the scene:

> **Puppet says:** *If I get double purple next time, I'll win. Oh wow, I got double purple!!*
>
> **Brainy takes a deep mindful breath and thinks aloud**: *I don't like to lose, but I know it's just a game, and I can squeeze and release my muscles to stay calm. If I stay calm, Paco will want to play with me again. Maybe I'll win next time!*
>
> **Brainy says:** *Good game, Paco! Would you like to play again?*
>
> **Puppet says:** *Good game, Brainy! Sure, it's fun to play with you!*

Review all the choices we have when playing a game, and how we can be mindful of our own and others' feelings to make the best choice possible when: choosing which game to play, choosing which color to use, choosing who goes first, and choosing how to react when we win or lose. When we remember that games are fun, and we think about how others feel, we can have more fun playing games together!

Thank the puppets, put them away, and move on to Kindness Pals.

 ## Kindness Pals

Explain that students will practice these skills with their Kindness Pals today while playing a simple game of Rock, Paper, Scissors.

Review these simple rules: Both children say "Rock, paper, scissors, go" and make their hands into a rock, a paper, or scissors at the word "go." Explain that rock beats scissors, paper beats rock, and scissors beat paper. Most children will likely be familiar with the game, although some may add in other symbols. Explain that they will only use those three symbols during play today. If there are students who do not know the game, be sure to pair them with a student who indicates they do know the game.

Pair up Kindness Pals, accounting for any absences, and give the following directions:

1. Sit with your pal in the listening position we've practiced: legs crossed, knees almost touching, shoulders pointing at each other.

2. Exchange friendly greetings.

3. When the teacher asks "who will go first?" both partners will say "You can!" In fact, in this game they will both go at the same time but it's good to practice saying the words "You can."

4. They will both say "rock, paper, scissors, go" and when they say "go," put their hands into one of the shapes. Changing their shape or waiting until they see their partner's shape is cheating and taking away the fun of the game. Remind them that losing is okay, it's just a game, and it's fun to play.

5. Both partners say "good game!" after determining who won, and then play again.

6. Repeat several times, until the signal is given that time is up.

7. Tell your pal goodbye and return to seats.

Closing: *The next time you play a game, try to use some of these kind choices you practiced today, and to remember that games are all about having fun. We'll tell about our games next time. See you then!*

Optional Lesson Extensions:

Books about Playing Games – Extend the concepts learned in class by reading stories about children playing games and dealing with losing, such as *Howard B. Wigglebottom Learns About Sportsmanship: Winning Isn't Everything* by Howard Binkow, or *Sally the Sore Loser: A Story About Winning and Losing* by Frank J. Sileo.

Class Call and Response – Use the "You can!" phrase as a call and response between teacher and students when a volunteer is needed for something that is not already assigned as a class job. For example, when the teacher wants a volunteer to show his work to the class, the teachers says "Class, who will show us your work first?" and the class says in unison "You can!" The teacher then picks someone. This eliminates everyone vying to be first and feeling disappointed when they are not chosen, by giving them a positive response and role to play. Remember, the more students practice desired skills, the more habit-forming they are likely to become!

Unit 6
Mindful Problem Solving

Mindfulness Skills – Visualization & Positive Self-Talk

Target quiet time during mindfulness ≅ 1 minute or longer

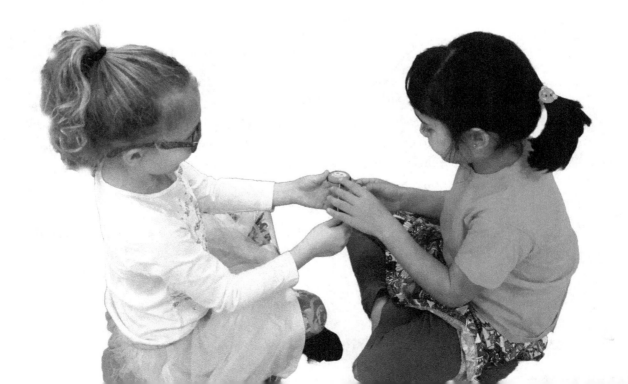

Week 26
How Big is My Problem?

OBJECTIVES: Use senses to visualize being in a calming place; categorize problems as small, medium, or large.

PREPARE: Bell or chime, thermometer picture from Week 8 and 23 (see Appendix)

Optional - a variety of simple "small problem" pictures gathered from clipart images, books, magazines, or other sources. Suggestions include:

- Someone falling down on grass or other relatively safe surface
- Losing a game
- Someone unable to go to a preferred center
- An empty marble jar (or whatever behavior management system the class uses)
- Not knowing how to do something in class
- Someone sticking out their tongue at you
- Not being able to wear the clothes you chose (this happens a lot with little ones!)
- Wanting a new toy at the store but parent says no
- Being told it's time to turn screens off

> ASCA Standards:

B-LS 1. Demonstrate critical-thinking skills to make informed decisions

B-SMS 7. Demonstrate effective coping skills when faced with a problem

TEACHING TIPS: As in other lessons that rely on 1-5 ratings, encourage children to use their fingers to participate and show what they think. Allowing everyone to participate simultaneously as much as possible is a great way to keep kids engaged and less frustrated because they don't get called on.

As long as children rate small problems as 0, 1, or 2 and larger problems as 4 or 5, don't worry about the differences between these numbers.

Children may see or experience "big" problems such as domestic violence, neighborhood violence, or homelessness. If this lesson brings up such questions for students, either connect them with the school counselor or talk with that student separately to affirm that they are dealing with some big problems, and acknowledge the big feelings that naturally go along with these problems. Be sure the child has someone to talk to regularly about these feelings, such as a teacher, nurse, social worker, or counselor.

Opening: *Hello fabulous friends! Did anyone play a game since I saw you last? Did you make kind choices that kept the game fun?*

Call on students who have something to share about playing games.

Mindfulness Practice

Say: *We have been practicing ways to calm our bodies. Today we will practice another strategy during our Mindful Moment. This strategy is called "imagination" or "visualization." When we imagine that our bodies are somewhere calm and relaxing, they usually feel that way even if we are not in that place. For me, a really relaxing place is near a pool, lake, or ocean. I like to feel the warm sun shining on me, and hear the water splashing, and that makes me feel very relaxed. Do you think you can try to imagine yourself in a relaxing place, too? Today we will all imagine we are outside in the sun near water, but you can make your water anywhere you want it to be. Some ideas are a stream, ocean, lake, or pool.*

Invite students to get in their mindful bodies and take three deep breaths. Ring the bell to indicate the start of the Mindful Moment, then model closing your eyes and placing hands in your lap.

After the sound stops, say: *With your eyes closed, let's use our senses to explore your imaginary place. First, "look" around your imaginary sunny spot. Notice the water, the color of the sky, and anything else you might see in your imagination around you.*

Next, use your sense of hearing to notice any sounds in your sunny spot, such as water splashing, birds tweeting, or something else.

Now let's use our sense of touch to notice what we feel. Is there sand underneath you, do you feel the warm sun shining on you, or you feel something else?

Finally, let's use our sense of smell to notice any particular smells in the air in our sunny spots. Do you smell saltwater, coconuts, or perhaps something else?

Now let's sit quietly and just enjoy being in our sunny spots for another few moments. Breathe in, breathe out, and relax.

After a period of quiet time, ring the bell again. After students raise their hands and open their eyes, invite them to share something they noticed in their sunny spots, and/or how their bodies feel after this exercise.

 Lesson

Say: *We have added belly breathing, body scanning, muscle relaxation, and today, imagination to our list of ways to calm our bodies down, or to bring a 5-size feeling down to a 1 or 2-size feeling. Now we are going to learn another strategy to add to our list: knowing how big or small our problem is. You see, just like we can give a number to describe our feelings, we can do the same for the size of our problem. All problems can have a number from 1-5, but many people get confused about the numbers. They think they are having a big, huge, 5-size problem, but really the problem is only a tiny 1 or 2-size problem.*

Remind the students of Paco's problem he had when he went to get a shot. Ask the students if they think that was a really huge 5-sized problem. Remind them to show you with their fingers (5 if they think it was big, 1 if small, or anything in between). Use this exercise as a quick visual assessment of students' understanding of the concepts taught in today's class.

Say: *Paco certainly thought getting shots was a big problem. But guess what? Although it may feel a little scary, getting shots is really not a big problem. I'm going to teach you today how to not get confused, like Paco and many people do, about problem sizes. There are two easy questions you have to answer about the problem:*

1. Is it dangerous? If not - it's a small problem! If it is – it's a bigger problem.

2. Does it last a long time? If not – it's a small problem! If it does – it's a bigger problem.

> TEACHING TIP: For older children a third question can be added: How many people have the problem? Just one usually means a smaller problem, while many typically means a bigger problem. With 4-6 year

olds, however, the first two questions are generally sufficient to teach the concept.

Say: *For Paco's problem, is getting a shot dangerous? Of course not, shots actually keep you healthy. Does a shot last a long time? Nope, it's over with in a second or two! So show me again on your fingers what size problem this is? Yes, it's a tiny problem!* [Most children should be able to show 0, 1 or 2 fingers this time.]

Encourage the children to continue thinking about the two questions and using their fingers to show what they think about the size of each of the following problems. Discuss some or all of the following problems or others you create based on real-life examples the students share, in random order. If available, use clipart pictures gathered ahead of time. If you will not be using pictures, describe each scenario orally.

Invite children to use their fingers to rate the problem. Then discuss the two questions until you mostly all agree on whether the problem is small (0, 1, or 2) or large (4 or 5).

- You are on vacation and hiking up a mountain when the mountain starts erupting - it is actually a volcano! You have to run quickly to get away. *Big problem, so big feelings and reactions are expected!*

- You are driving down a road when the ground begins to shake, and the road splits apart right in front of you! You have to stop the car and carefully get out and get to safety. *Big problem, so big feelings and reactions are expected!*

- You are riding your bike/trike/scooter, wearing a helmet and pads, and you fall over onto the grass. *Small problem, dust the grass off and get back on the bike!*

- You are playing a favorite game with a friend but are about to lose. *Small problem, just say "good game" and ask if the friend wants to play again.* Use Brainy to model thinking how it's not dangerous and doesn't last long, so staying calm is best. Say "good game" and ask to play again.

- You are really excited to choose your favorite center, but it's full. *Small problem, just wait until someone leaves that center and then you can choose it.*

- You earned no marbles in your jar today (or whatever behavior management system the class uses). *Small problem, you will have to try again tomorrow!*

- You are having trouble understanding the workbook page and don't know what to do. *Small problem, ask the teacher for help.*

- Your mom or dad wouldn't let you wear the clothes you really wanted to wear to school today (too cold for shorts, clothes too dirty, and so on). *Small problem, you can wear it when you get home or another day.*

Continue discussing these or other problems the students name or regularly encounter. If you are using pictures to go along with the problems, you can sort them into small and large at either end of the thermometer. Spread them out in the middle of the circle so everyone can see there are many small problems and only 1-2 large ones. Eventually someone will usually point this out, or ask "Why do we only have 1 big problem but there are so many small ones? This leads to the closing discussion.

Say: *Why do you think we talked about so many small problems today, and only a few big problems?* **Take suggestions**. *Most of our problems are very small, and bigger problems are rare- they don't happen very often. Try to remember that the next time you are having a problem; it's most likely to be a small problem and not a big one.*

 Kindness Pals

Pair up partners, account for any absences, and then give the following instructions:

1. Sit with your pal in the listening position we've practiced: legs crossed, knees almost touching, shoulders pointing at each other.
2. Exchange friendly greetings.
3. Choose one partner to tell about a recent problem.
4. Both partners think through the questions to decide what size problem it was and what a matching reaction would be.
5. The partner who told about a problem now tells whether their reaction matched the size of the problem, or whether they got confused and had a bigger reaction than necessary.
6. Repeat with the other partner.
7. Make sure both partners get a chance to tell about one problem, and continue as time allows.
8. Give your pal a friendly goodbye and return to the circle.

Closing: *Try to notice any problems you have during the next week, and whether they are small, medium, or large. We'll tell about it next time. See you then!*

Optional Lesson Extensions for Problem Sizes:

Class Poster – Create a class poster that shows the problem-size thermometer and the criteria: danger, how long it lasts, how many people are affected (if introduced) in a visual way. Consider taking photos of students role-playing different problems that may arise in the classroom on a regular basis. As conflicts or other small problems occur, invite students to refer to the Problem-Size poster.

Tattling versus telling – The problem size concept can also help students understand the difference between tattling and telling. When a problem is bigger and someone might get hurt, the problem needs to be reported to the teacher. Most small problems can be worked out and the teacher doesn't usually need to be notified. Tattling is usually some form of small problems being reported to the teacher on a regular basis.

Optional Lesson Extension for Visualization:

Drawing – After the visualization activity, give children blank paper on which to illustrate their relaxing spot. Be sure to guide children through each sense used in the activity: draw what you see, hear, touch, and smell.

Week 27
What Is A Conflict?

OBJECTIVES: Use visualization as a strategy for self-calming; identify conflicts as small problems between two or more people.

PREPARE: Bell or chime, puppets, new Kindness Pal list

> ASCA Standards:

B-SS 2. Create positive and supportive relationships with other students

B-SS 6. Use effective collaboration and cooperation skills

TEACHING TIPS: If students can notice they are having a conflict, they are much more likely to be able to resolve it quickly. The small pause it takes to notice, or be mindful of, the current conflict often provides the space to think before reacting in anger.

Mindfulness Practice

Say: *We have been practicing ways to calm our bodies. Today we will practice using our imagination again. This is also called "visualization" because we use our sense of vision to "see" something in our brains, even if we don't "see" it in real life. So if you hear me or someone else say we are "visualizing," that's just a fancy word for using our imaginations!*

Last week we all imagined we were in a sunny spot. Today, you can choose to imagine yourself in the same spot or somewhere completely different that makes you feel relaxed. Maybe your room at home, or a relative's house, the reading corner in your classroom, or somewhere else. Choose a place that is your very own calm spot.

Invite students to get in their mindful bodies and take three deep breaths. Ring the bell to indicate the start of the Mindful Moment, then model closing your eyes and placing hands in your lap.

After the sound stops, **say**: *With your eyes closed, let's use our senses to explore your imaginary relaxing place. First, "look" around you. Notice the colors and objects you see. Notice anything else you might see in your calm place around you.*

Next, use your sense of hearing to notice any sounds you hear in your relaxing place, such as music playing, your heart beating, or something else.

Now let's use our sense of touch to notice what we feel. Is there something soft underneath you, is there a blanket or something else you are touching?

Finally, let's use our sense of smell to notice any particular smells in our relaxing spots. Do you smell cookies baking, a soft perfume, or something else?

Now let's sit quietly and just enjoy being in our relaxing spots for another few moments. Breathe in, breathe out, and relax.

After a period of quiet time, ring the bell again. After students raise their hands and open their eyes, invite them to share something they noticed in their relaxing spots, and/or how their bodies feel after this exercise.

Call on all who have something to share about their visualization experience.

> TEACHING TIP: Often children are excited to tell about off-topic events or situations, such as a lost tooth, a birthday, or a special outing, even if it's not the right time to do so. Try to encourage these to wait until the end of class, but responding to some of these in the middle of class will be unavoidable. Simply smile, say "Wow, great news!" and move quickly on to the next person.

Sometimes children intentionally provide silly answers to your questions, which can set off a string of silliness (a "silly string") of similar answers. When this occurs, give as little attention to the silly answer as possible (make no comment, keep a neutral face) and move on to the next hand raise, giving praise to the next non-silly answer.

 Lesson

Say: *We have learned about knowing the size of our problem, and ways to stay calm when we have a problem. Today we will be talking about a problem we all have sometimes that starts out very small. If we don't try to fix the problem, it can get bigger and bigger. The problem is called a "conflict." Does anyone know what the word "conflict" means?*

Call on students to share, and then give the following definition:

Conflict is when two or more people argue or disagree about something.

Use Paco and Brainy to model the following skit. Make sure the children know the puppets are *acting*, or *pretending* during this skit, since they are used to seeing them be very friendly with each other.

Put the bell or another handy object (marker, eraser, pencil, and so on) between the puppets. Have each one insist they need to use it first. Continue arguing back and forth until Amygdala starts screaming and yelling and the puppets tussle over the object.

Say: *That was a conflict over who got to use the* (object) *first. Let's think about the size of the problem using the two questions we learned. Was it dangerous? Not at first, but when the puppets started grabbing and pushing it started to become unsafe. Did the problem last a long time or a little time? Well, they still haven't worked out who will use the* (object) *first, so it's still going on. Since this conflict was getting unsafe, and it wasn't over with quickly, it is now a bigger problem. This is how a tiny problem can become a big one if we don't do something about it.*

> TEACHING TIP: Students will also be eager to share personal conflicts experienced recently, once they understand what the word means. Encourage them to wait to share their stories with their Kindness Pal in a few minutes.

Explain that there are many different kinds of conflicts. Some arguments are over an object, like the puppets just showed. Some are about whose turn it is, or wanting to do something we are told we can't do, or even about teasing and name-calling.

Use the puppets to act out a few more simple conflicts students might have in school. Examples include:

- Getting in front of someone in line
- Someone bumping another person with their body
- One person telling the other person they don't like their drawing

Begin to explore ideas the students have on how to resolve these conflicts, as they will naturally want to name what the puppets could or should do when you model the conflicts. Listen to ideas and try to incorporate these into the next lessons about tools to resolve conflicts.

Kindness Pals

Today assign new Kindness Pals, reminding students to say "okay." Partner students with each other, account for any absences, and then give the following instructions:

1. Sit with your pal in the listening position
    we've practiced: legs crossed, knees almost touching, shoulders pointing at each other.
2. Give your new pal a friendly greeting or several, followed by a compliment.
3. Tell about a conflict or argument you had with someone.
4. Tell whether the problem stayed small, or it went on and became a bigger problem.
5. If both pals have shared one problem and they still have more time, they can each share another problem.
6. Tell your pal goodbye and return to the circle.

Closing: *If you have any conflicts, or small problems with another person, try to notice whether the problem stays small or gets bigger. We'll tell about our experiences next time. See you then!*

Optional Lesson Extensions:

Video - *Sesame Street's "Word of the Day is Conflict"* – show this short video with Robin Williams and the two-headed monster. Pause the video after the monster attempts to show "conflict" and discuss whether this is or is not conflict and why. After the video is done, encourage students to share times they had a conflict with someone, what it was about, and how it was resolved.

Book – *The Zax* in *The Sneetches and Other Stories* by Dr. Seuss. Read this short story and discuss the conflict the two Zax have. Questions you may want to ask:

How did the conflict keep getting bigger?

Did the Zax ever solve the conflict?

What simple ways might they have solved the conflict quickly?

Week 28
My Toolbox

OBJECTIVES: Use visualization as a method of self-calming; define and apply the concept of tools as ways to solve conflicts.

PREPARE: Bell or chime, puppets

> ASCA Standards:

B-SS 2. Create positive and supportive relationships with other students

B-SS 6. Use effective collaboration and cooperation skills

Opening: *Hello precious people! Did you notice yourself or someone else having a conflict since I saw you last? If you did, let's hear about it now.*

Call on several students to share experiences with recent conflicts.

 Mindfulness Practice

Say: *We have been practicing ways to calm our bodies. Today is the last time we will practice using our imagination, or "visualization."*

Today, you can choose to imagine yourself in the same spot as last week, or you can choose somewhere completely different that makes you feel relaxed. Maybe your bed in your room, being hugged by someone you love, or somewhere else. Choose a place that is your very own calm spot.

Invite students to get in their mindful bodies and take three deep breaths. Ring the bell to indicate the start of the Mindful Moment, then model closing your eyes and placing hands in your lap.

After the sound stops, **say**: *With your eyes closed, let's use our senses to explore your imaginary relaxing place. First, "look" around you. Notice the colors and objects you see. Notice anything else you might see in your calm place around you.*

Next, use your sense of hearing to notice any sounds you hear in your relaxing place, such as music playing, your heart beating, or something else.

Now let's use our sense of touch to notice what we feel. Is there something soft underneath you? Is there a blanket or something else you are touching?

Finally, let's use our sense of smell to notice any particular smells in our relaxing spots. Do you smell cookies baking, a soft perfume, or something else?

Now let's sit quietly and just enjoy being in our relaxing spots for another few moments. Breathe in, breathe out, and relax.

After a period of quiet time, ring the bell again. After students raise their hands and open their eyes, invite them to share something they noticed in their relaxing spots, and/or how their bodies feel after this exercise.

Call on all who have something to share about their visualization experience.

 Lesson

Say: *Who knows what a tool is? What do we use tools for?*

Take suggestions from the students. They might name some common tools such as a hammer, saw, or screwdriver. Encourage students to think about what is happening when someone uses a tool: **they are building or fixing something that is broken.**

Say: *Last week we learned about conflicts, and how they are arguments or disagreements between people. Today we are going to start learning about ways to fix a conflict using some special tools. Our tools will not be hammers and saws, but just like hammers and saws our tools will help us fix something. They will help us* **fix our conflicts and build friendships!**

> TEACHING TIP: While it can be beneficial to have young children act in role-plays, I have not found it generally beneficial to have them act out conflicts or other misbehaviors. In a whole-class setting without much preparation, children can get very silly quickly and enjoy acting out the "wrong" way a little too much. If you do not have time to structure the setting and establish clear ground rules and procedures for role-plays, instead have students correct your behavior and/or model the correct behavior that you or the puppet should show.

Role Play #1

Use the puppets or two students to model the following conflict: they want to play cards, but one really wants to play Go Fish, while the other wants to play Slapjack, or any other game the students are familiar with. They begin to argue about which game to play, which is more fun, who got to pick last time, and so on. Clearly they are forgetting that games are for having fun, and are getting stuck in a conflict instead!

Stop them and ask if they have ever heard of the word **compromise**. Explain that a compromise means the people who are having a conflict each get some of what they want, though they may not get everything they want.

Ask the class what each person wants (to play the preferred game), and how they could each get a little of what they want in this case. There are many different ways to compromise, or make sure both people get some of what they want.

Likely responses include: **take turns** playing the games each wants, **combine** the games into a slap/go fish game, or **do something else** they both like. Then have the students/puppets model all of these options.

Guide students in this type of dialogue:

> **Student #1 says**: *I really want to play Go Fish with the cards today!*

> **Student #2 says**: *Well, I really wanted to play Slap Jack with the cards!*

> **Both students begin arguing over which game is better, more fun, etc.**

Student #1 says: *Wait! I think we're having a conflict! Let's take some deep breaths and think about a tool we can use to help us. Let's try **taking turns** to fix this conflict! We can play your game for a little while, then we can switch and play my game for a little while. That way we both get to play the games we really wanted!*

Student #2 says: *Oh, that's a good idea. We both get to play our games and have fun together!*

Point out that Student #1 was making a kind choice by offering to play Student #2's game first in the compromise. Student #1 was thinking about Student #2's feelings. Kind behavior solves conflicts very quickly. In fact, when people speak mindfully and make kind choices, they don't have many conflicts at all!

Remind the students that games are for fun, and ultimately both children wanted to have fun playing with each other. Compromising helped them work out their conflict pretty quickly. **Repeat** the skit with the same or different students, using the "combination" and "choose something different" tools. Be sure to have students model taking a Mindful Moment with a few deep breaths before selecting a tool.

Say: *Those are all great conflict tools. Class, let's put "**take turns**," "**share**," and "**do something else**" into our imaginary toolbox!*

Model opening a box and placing the tools inside, then closing it again with your hands.

Role Play #2

Review using these tools with a different conflict. Two people want to read the same book, like Paco and Brainy last week both wanted to use the same object. Use the puppets, or select two students, to role play this for the class. Ask how they can use one of the tools we just named to each get some of what they want.

They can **take turns** using the object so they both get to use it. They can **share** the object and use it at the same time. They can **do something else**. Model one or all three of these tools.

Guide students in this type of dialogue:

> **Student #1:** *I can't wait to read the new dinosaur book we got in our class library! I'm going to get it now that we have free reading time.*

> **Student #2:** *I already called it! I said I was going to read it today during free reading time! Hmm. This might be a conflict. I know, let's have a Mindful Moment and take some deep breaths together. Both students model this. How about we **share** the book and look at it together?*

> **Student #1:** *Okay, that way we both will get to read it today. Good idea!*

Say: *Those are all great conflict tools. Class, let's put "**take turns**," "**share**," and "**do something else**" into our imaginary toolbox!*

Model opening a box and placing the tools inside, then closing it again with your hands.

Say: *Which part of our brains helps us remember our conflict tools when we need them? Yes, our hippocampus! And which part of our brains helps us choose and use one of the tools? Right, our PFC! We will talk a little more about conflicts now with our Kindness Pals.*

 Kindness Pals

Partner students with each other, account for any absences, and then give the following instructions:

1. Sit with your pal in the listening position we've practiced: legs crossed, knees almost touching, shoulders pointing at each other.

2. Exchange friendly greetings.

3. See if you and your pal can name the two tools we learned about today. What are some of the different ways we can make sure both people get some of what they want?

4. Tell about a time you used one of these tools when you had a conflict. Did it help you fix the conflict?

5. Tell your pal goodbye and return to the circle.

Closing: *Try to remember to take a Mindful Moment and use these tools anytime you notice conflicts, and we'll tell about it next time. See you then!*

Optional Lesson Extensions:

Books – *The Day No One Played Together: A Story About Compromise* by Donalisa Helsley. Read this picture book about two sisters who have trouble deciding what game to play.

Art Project – Collect small shoe boxes or tissue boxes to create Conflict Toolboxes with your students. Each student can decorate the outside of their toolbox, and can draw representations of the tools to go inside. Students can continue adding tools to their boxes in the next lesson.

Week 29
More Tools for Conflicts

OBJECTIVES: Use positive self-talk as a method of self-calming; define and apply three conflict resolution strategies to address common problems students may have in school.

PREPARE: Bell or chime

> ASCA Standards:

B-SS 6. Use effective collaboration and cooperation skills

B-SMS 7. Demonstrate effective coping skills when faced with a problem

Opening: *Hi awesome amigos! Did anyone use one of the tools to solve a conflict with someone else? Please tell me about it!*

Teaching Tip: Remind children to refrain from naming people when talking about a conflict, and instead to say "someone did x" or "a person said z". Saying that person's name out loud in front of them and others isn't usually a kind choice!

Call on several students to share their conflicts AND the way they resolved them. Respond with encouraging statements to all who share their attempts to use a strategy to help resolve a conflict.

Mindfulness Practice

Say: *Today during our Mindful Moment we are going to learn one more important way to calm ourselves. It is called "positive self-talk." Does anyone here ever talk to yourself? Well, we are going to practice talking to ourselves today and telling ourselves some very good, or <u>positive</u>, words we might forget at times. Who can name some nice words you like to hear someone say to you?*

Call on students to share. Encourage them to think big: I like you, you're awesome, you're a rock star, you're so nice and kind, and so on. **Guide them** through a practice saying several of these phrases aloud, pointing to their chests as they do so.

Say: *Those were amazing positive statements! Now, what would you say to someone who was having a big feeling, perhaps getting angry or very upset about something that is happening, to help them feel better?*

Call on students to share. Suggestions may include mindfulness practices such as taking deep breaths, sending heartfulness to yourself, using another calming strategy; noticing the size of the problem; or using one of the conflict tools.

Say: *These are all very good strategies! Now I'd like to tell you about one more:* positive self-talk.

If I were feeling angry, and someone said those positive words to me, they probably would help me feel better and remind me I can do something about my feelings. Let's try it with ourselves now. Go ahead and tell yourself some of these positive words.

Now, we will give ourselves positive statements, or words, like these during our mindfulness practice today. Are you ready?

> TEACHING TIP: Remind students about their thought bubbles, and they can "talk" to themselves using their thought bubbles rather than aloud during the Mindful Moment. If students forget and talk aloud that's okay! Ask them if they can try to whisper instead of speak aloud.

Instruct students to get in their mindful bodies and take three deep breaths. Ring the bell to indicate the start of the Mindful Moment. After the sound stops, model closing your eyes and placing hands in your lap.

Say: *Now, let's pretend that you are looking at yourself when you might be upset or just not feeling great, and speak to that self. Tell yourself "I'm okay," (pause) "I can do this," (pause) "I am awesome!" (pause) Give yourself some more positive words right now, whichever words you choose. Then I'll ring the bell in a few moments.*

After a period of quiet time, ring the bell again. After students raise a hand and open their eyes, invite them to share something they said to themselves during this time. Discuss how positive self-talk may or may not feel different from Heartfulness for oneself as practiced in Week 13.

 Lesson

Say: *Last week, we learned that a tool is something that helps us adjust, fix, or build something. Our toolbox already has several important tools in it, and today we're going to add some more tools we can use to help us during conflicts.*

Review the tools discussed in the previous lesson, if needed: **take turns, share, and do something else.**

Say: *The next tool we're going to add is also one we've talked about before. It's called **Others First,** or letting someone else do something they really want. We called it making a kind choice. Remember when Paco and Brainy both wanted to go to the Lego center, and one made a kind choice to let the other go since there was just one spot left? We always have the option of thinking about how others feel and making a kind choice to give someone what they really want, especially if it's not that big of a deal to us. That's the Others First tool. Let's try that in a role-play now.*

Guide students in this type of dialogue:

Role Play #1 – Two students are both thirsty and get to the water fountain at about the same time. They begin to argue about who got there first, and then one student remembers the **Others First tool.**

> **Student #1** – *Oh, I'm SO thirsty, I really neeeeed some water now!*
>
> **Student #2** – *Me too, I'm going to be first to the water fountain. I'm SO thirsty I could drink a gallon!*
>
> **Student #1** – *But I said it first! I'm going to run so fast I'll beat you there!*
>
> **Student #2** – (talks to self) *Oh no, I'm starting to feel angry about this, but I don't want to have a meltdown since it's a kind of small problem. Take some deep breaths. Okay self, you can DO this! (Now speaks aloud) You know what? I think we might get in a conflict at the water fountain. I'm going to walk and let you get there first, since you're really thirsty. I'm thirsty, too, but I can wait a few more minutes. Go ahead!*
>
> **Student #1** – *Wow, thanks! That was kind of you.*
>
> **Student #2** – *You're welcome!*

Discuss this tool with the class, and how positive self-talk can help us remember our tools and choose one when we might need it. Point out that when students make kind choices like these, others feel good about that student and are more likely to want to be around him or her. This is another benefit of using the Others First tool!

Tips for using the Others First tool:
- Think about how others feel
- Don't insist on being first
- Consider letting the other person have what he/she wants

Model opening a box and placing the kindness tool inside, then closing it again with your hands.

Say: *There's another tool we will add next, and it's called **look for more**. Look for more works best when two people are in a conflict about something they both want or need to use. It could have also worked for our water fountain skit, too!*

Role Play #2: Two students both need to use the red marker to complete a drawing. They begin arguing over the marker, until one remembers they can **look for more.**

Student #1: *Can you pass me the red marker? I need it for my flowers.*

Student #2: *Nope, I'm using it to finish my fire engine. I'm going to be using it for a while. It's a really big engine!*

Student #1: *Oh, come on! You've been using it for a long time already. It's my turn to have it now! (Takes some deep, mindful breaths and thinks to self) Ok, I'm feeling some hotness in my face. That usually means I'm getting angry. I notice my tummy getting tight. I can stay calm right now, there is probably a tool that can help me with this conflict. (Speaks aloud) Hey, can't we **look for more** red markers?*

Student #2: *Oh yeah, I think there are some more in the supplies shelf. I'll go get you one now.*

Student #1: *Thank you!*

Review other times this tool might be useful, and act those out if time allows. You may also choose to **review other tools** that might also work in these scenarios.

Say: *Our toolbox now has five powerful tools you can use when there is a conflict:*

Tool #1 – Take turns or combine ideas

Tool #2 - Share it

Tool #3 – Do something else

Tool #4 – Others first

Tool #5 - Look for more

Say: *I want to tell you about one more tool you can put in your conflict toolbox. Have you ever heard of having a backup plan, or "Plan B?" A backup plan is what you do in case your first idea doesn't work out. It's always important to have a Plan B for backup. If you are having a conflict and you've tried using the all of the tools you can remember, but the conflict still isn't fixed, I want you to know the backup plan. Our backup tool is always this: get a grown-up to help you. Now let's put that tool in our toolbox, too!*

Backup Tool – Get a grown-up's help

Model opening a box and placing the tool inside, then closing it again with your hands.

 ### Kindness Pals

Today's Kindness Pal time will be used to practice these tools during three scenarios. Partner students with each other, account for any absences, and then give the following instructions:

1. Sit with your pal in the listening position we've practiced: legs crossed, knees almost touching, shoulders pointing at each other.
2. Exchange friendly greetings.
3. Open your imaginary toolboxes and tell each other about all six tools you have.
4. Practice using the backup tool by pretending your partner is a grown-up, and ask each other to help you.
5. Tell your pal goodbye and return to the circle.

Closing: *Try to use one or more of these tools the next time you're having a conflict, and we'll tell about it next time. See you then!*

Optional Lesson Extensions:

Class Tool Book – Take pictures of students modeling the conflict resolution strategies practiced in these lessons and others they can think of. Put these into a class book labeled "Ways to Fix Conflicts" and keep in the classroom for student reference.

Art Project – Continue adding these tools to the Conflict Toolboxes with your students. Each student can decorate the outside of their toolbox, and can draw representations of the tools to go inside.

Week 30
Heroes

OBJECTIVES: Practice positive self-talk as a method of self-calming; demonstrate advocating for others who are being teased or picked on.

PREPARE: Bell or chime, puppets, new Kindness Pal list

> ASCA Standards:

B-SS 2. Create positive and supportive relationships with other students

B-SS 8. Demonstrate advocacy skills and the ability to assert self when necessary

TEACHING TIP: Bullying is more serious than a simple conflict between two students. If students mention the word bullying, you may need to make a distinction during this lesson. Bullying involves three components:

1) Repeated actions that are done more than once
2) Actions that are purposely done to hurt feelings or body
3) Some type of power difference

Most conflicts and teasing among 4-6 year olds does not include a power difference, and is not often done with intention to hurt someone. Therefore, the majority of problems between children this age are some form of misunderstanding or other peer conflicts. It is possible, however, that some repeated and cruel teasing can also be bullying behaviors.

Opening: *Hello wonderful ones! Did anyone use positive self-talk to help you stay calm and remember your tools during a conflict? If you did, I'd love to hear about it!*

Call on several students to share their experiences.

 Mindfulness Practice

Say: *We're going to practice positive self-talk one more time today during our Mindful Moment. Who can name some positive words you like to hear said to you?*

Call on students to share. Remind them to think big: I like you, you're awesome, you're a rock star, you're so nice and kind, and so on. Have them practice saying these phrases aloud, pointing to their chests as they do so.

Say: *Those were amazing positive statements! Now, what would you say to someone who was having a big feeling, perhaps getting angry or very upset about something that is happening, to help them feel better?*

Call on students to share. Suggestions may include: take deep breaths, send kind thoughts to yourself, ask yourself how big a problem it really is, use one of your calming strategies, use one of your conflict tools, and so on.

Say: *If I were feeling angry, and someone said those words to me, they probably would help me feel better. Now we will give ourselves positive statements like these during our mindfulness practice today. Are you ready?*

Instruct students to get in their mindful bodies and take three deep breaths. Ring the bell to indicate the start of the Mindful Moment. After the sound stops, model closing your eyes and placing hands in your lap.

Say: *Now pretend that you are looking at yourself, when you may be upset or just not feeling great, and speak to yourself. Tell yourself "I'm okay," (pause) "I can do this," (pause) "I am awesome!" (pause) Give yourself some more positive talk right now. Then I'll ring the bell in a few moments.*

After a period of quiet time, ring the bell again. After students raise their hands and open their eyes, invite them to share something they said to themselves during this time. Discuss how this may or may not feel different from Heartfulness for oneself, practiced in Week 13.

 Lesson

Say: *Today we will be discussing heroes. What is a hero? Who knows what that word means?* You will likely hear some or all of the following:

- Someone who saves people
- Someone who is brave
- Someone who faces danger
- Someone who helps people when they need it most
- Batman, Spiderman, Wonder Woman, and so on

Next, ask these questions to the class:

Can you be a hero?

How do you help people when they really need it?

Remind students that we've been learning how to deal with conflicts in past weeks. Explain that they all have a "superpower" and it is knowing many ways to fix conflicts. Refer to the list of tools created in the previous week.

Say: *Sometimes kids like to tease someone. That's different than a usual conflict where two people are arguing about something. When someone teases, there's not always a conflict or argument happening. Who knows what it means to tease someone?*

Take suggestions on what teasing means from the students. Then provide this simple definition: teasing means making mean comments to someone, calling them unkind names, and pointing out differences in an unkind way. This is NOT a typical conflict, and needs a special tool.

> TEACHING TIP: When discussing teasing, it may be helpful to distinguish this from familial nicknames, words that rhyme with your name, or other words said in a friendly way. One way to tell the difference is to think about the person saying the words. If that is a person who loves you or cares about you a lot (relatives, friends, or other special people) then most likely the words are not intended to hurt feelings but rather to show care and affection. This can often be hard for young children with still-developing perspective-taking skills to distinguish, which is why it's good to make a point of mentioning it here.

Say: *When someone is saying or doing something unkind, the special tool we can use is called Speak Up. We can say "Stop, I don't like that!"*

Invite the students to hold up a hand while saying this phrase, and then add it to your list.

Teasing Tool – Speak up
- Tell someone to stop
- Use firm words
- Tell them how it makes one feel

Say: *So far, we've only talked about using tools for yourself when <u>you</u> are the person having a conflict. But have you ever noticed <u>someone else</u> getting teased? How can we use what we've learned with others who may need our help?*

Model using the "Stop!" phrase in situations with others.

Say: *Hold up your palm, look at the person who is being unkind to someone else, and firmly say "Stop, that is unkind!" You may also want to say some of your positive statements to the person who was getting teased. "I think you're awesome!" might help make that person feel much better.*

Use two students or the puppets to demonstrate:

> **Student #1**: *Hi, how are you?*

> **Student #2:** *I'm not doing so well. Some other kids were just teasing me. They said words like "Hey, you're so slow! You lost the race at recess and now we're going to call you slow-poke from now on!"*

> **Student #1:** *Well that wasn't kind at all! Where are those kids? I'm going to go talk to them right now!*

> **Student #2:** *They're over there. (Gesture to another part of the room.)*

> **Student #1:** *(moves in that direction) Hey, I heard you were calling my friend "slow poke." Did you know she feels sad when you do that? You need to stop, it's unkind and hurting my friend's feelings!*

> **You say:** *Wow, you are a HERO for speaking up when your friend was being teased like that! I'm so proud of you!*

> **Student #2:** *Yes, thank you so much! It means a lot to me to know you are my friend, even if those kids are not being kind to me right now.*

> **Student #1:** *Well, I just want you to know I think you're awesome! You lost that race but you can do lots of other things kids can't do.*

> **Student #2:** *Wow, thanks for saying those positive words. They really help me feel better.*

> **Student #1:** *You're welcome!*

Ask if all people can do what these kids did. Of course they can! Anyone can speak up for someone who is getting teased, and then say kind words to the person getting teased. Anyone who uses their "superpower" of helping others is a hero. A hero can be a boy or a girl.

Remind students of the "Plan B" tool learned last week, in case they feel scared or unsure about speaking to the kids doing the teasing or acting unkind. It is

OK to be fearful they might start teasing you, and if that is the case then use the backup plan to tell an adult. In fact, if you have to speak up for someone else it's a good idea to always let an adult know. Model this with the students or puppets as an alternative.

Puppet: *Hi Brainy, how are you?*

Brainy: *I'm not doing so well, Paco. Some other kids were just teasing me. They said words like "Hey, Brainy, you're so slow! You lost the race at recess and so we're going to call you "slow poke" from now on!"*

Puppet: *Well that wasn't kind at all! I'm going to tell the teacher about it right now. Mr. Teacher, did you know some kids are teasing and being mean to Brainy by calling him "slow poke?"*

Say: (Responding as the teacher) *Oh, no I didn't know that and I'll go talk to them right now. Thanks, Paco for letting me know. I'll take care of it. You're a good friend to Brainy.*

Puppet: *Brainy, I just want you to know I think you're awesome! You lost that race but you can do lots of other things kids can't do.*

Brainy: *Wow, thanks for saying those positive words, Paco. They really help me feel better.*

Puppet: *You're welcome!*

Put away the puppets and move to Kindness Pals, where students will each get to practice speaking up for others.

Kindness Pals

Assign new Kindness Pals today. These are the last official pals of the curriculum rotations. Today Kindness Pals will work together to practice using their superpowers of helping each other. Partner students with each other, account for any absences, and then give the following instructions:

1. Sit with your new pal in the listening position we've practiced: legs crossed, knees almost touching, shoulders pointing at each other.
2. Give your new pal friendly greetings, followed by a compliment.

3. Pretend you overheard someone teasing your pal.

4. Say "Stop! That is not kind to do/say."

5. Then tell your pal something positive, like the positive words we've been saying to ourselves during the Mindful Moment.

6. Make sure both partners get a turn to talk.

7. Tell your pal goodbye and return to the circle.

Closing: *Try to use your hero superpowers of helping others and dealing with teasing, and we'll tell about it next time. See you then!*

Optional Lesson Extensions:

Art Activity – Use a badge template (widely available online) to have students design their own superhero badge. You can also use this as a reinforcement when children speak up for others, by allowing that student to make a hero badge for themselves. See if students can write the word "Stop!" on their badges. If not, help write it for them. If possible, help children cut out their badges and tape to their shirts for the rest of the day.

Books – There are many books about dealing with friend conflicts, such as *The Berenstain Bears and the Trouble With Friends* by Stan Berenstain, *The Recess Queen* by Alexis O'Neill and Laura Huliska-Beith, and *A Children's Book About Teasing* by Joy Berry. Read these or other similar books to the class to further discussions on name calling and how to respond when someone is teased. Stop and ask students to consider which tool would be best to use in each scenario. Encourage children to use their hero superpowers to help the student getting teased.

Mindfulness Skill – Student Choice

Target quiet time during mindfulness ≅ 1 minute or longer

Week 31
Peace Is...

OBJECTIVES: Synthesize concepts learned throughout the year to form a sensory-based definition of peace.

PREPARE: Bell or chime; one "Peace" booklet per student (see Appendix)

Optional Materials: Peaceful sounds (bell, music, ocean waves, and so on); peaceful smells (mint, lemon, vanilla, dryer sheet, and so on). It works best to put these in a container or sandwich bag that can be passed around from student to student to smell.

> ASCA Standards:

B-LS 2. Demonstrate creativity

B-SS 1. Use effective oral and written communication skills and listening skills

TEACHING TIP: This is a longer, optional final project that may need to be broken up over several days.

Opening: *Hello happy heroes! Did anyone get to practice their superpower hero skills by speaking up for someone else? Did you say any positive words to yourself or someone else this week?*

Call on students to share their experiences.

 Mindfulness Practice

Say: *Wow, class, we have learned so much over this whole year, and we are almost at the end of our time together. During our Mindful Moments we've learned about and practiced:*

Mindfulness Practice
- Belly breathing and other ways to take deep breaths
- Noticing our feelings and thoughts
- Practicing heartfulness and feeling thankful for others
- Using our five senses very deeply to notice more around us
- Scanning every part of our bodies and relaxing our muscles
- Using our imaginations to pretend to be in a calming place
- Using positive self-talk and heartfulness to tell ourselves kind and encouraging words

Say: *We also learned about what it means to have a choice, and that our pre-frontal cortex helps us make choices. Today during the Mindful Moment, you will have the power to choose the activity that feels good to you. When I ring the bell, listen until it stops and then choose to do one or more of the skills we practiced this year. I'm going to be quiet so you can be mindful all on your own. After I ring the bell a second time, we'll raise our hands, open our eyes, and tell what mindfulness activity we chose to use today.*

Invite students to get in their mindful bodies. Take three deep breaths together. Ring the bell once, and close your eyes and place hands in your lap.

After a sustained period of quiet time, ring the bell again. Raise one hand, open your eyes, and invite children to share which mindfulness activities they chose today.

Say: *I'm so proud of you for being able to choose your own way to practice mindfulness. Since our **Peace of Mind** classes are almost finished, it will be important for you to know how to have a Mindful Moment on your own after school is over for the year.*

 Lesson

Say: *All year long we've been having "**Peace of Mind**" class. You know when you go to Art class you will be learning about drawing and painting. When you go to Music class you will be learning about different kinds of music. But what have we learned in **Peace of Mind** class? Peace can be a difficult idea to describe, because we can't all see and hear the same "Peace" like we can all see a painting or hear a song. Peace can mean different things to different people.*

In our very first lesson we talked about peace...do you remember? Paco thought we were saying "piece of pizza." We said then that peace is "very calm and without arguing or fighting." Have we learned how to be very calm? Have we learned how to work out problems so they don't become big fights and arguments?

Say: *To help us think about what we've learned, we will create a booklet about Peace. Everyone's booklet will be different, because peace is different to everyone and we can't all "see" the same peace.*

Remind students of the unit on Mindful Senses. Today we will use our five senses to try to describe the concept of Peace. Facilitate a discussion about each of the following:

- Peace looks like - Show or remind the students of peaceful images; children playing together, shaking hands, saying "you can," and so on. Use students to model some of these peaceful images.

- Peace sounds like - Think about our mindful listening activities. What sounds remind them of peace? You can ring the bells, play soft music, or ask for other examples of peaceful sounds. (Some will say "no sound" and you can write the word "quiet" instead.)

- Peace smells like – Recall the smells that were used during the Mindful Smells lesson. Invite students to think about what smells they like and those that invoke peace. If desired, bring back some of the items used during the Mindful Smells lesson.

- Peace tastes like - Foods that make you feel calm and peaceful, or maybe this is not a food item at all. A student may choose to draw clouds, for example, because they think clouds might taste peaceful.

- Peace feels like - Invite students to think about how their body feels when we practice mindfulness, when they are calm, and when they feel peaceful. Do they feel peace in a particular part of their body? How can they draw that? Alternately, if there was a sensation students particularly liked from the Mindful Touch lesson, they can draw that.

After discussing the above points, distribute the Peace booklets for students to illustrate.

> TEACHING TIP: If you are breaking this lesson into multiple sessions, have children only complete the pages for that sense immediately afterwards. For example, play several soothing sounds, smell some items, and look at some pictures. Then go to tables and complete the pages on hearing, smelling, and seeing Peace. You can collect the booklets and redistribute in the next class session, until all parts are completed.

Depending on how much time you have, choose any or all of the following closing activities.

- Play popcorn* to have students come up and share their Peace books with the class.

- Pair students with their Kindness Pal to show each other's Peace Books and give each other compliments on their books.

- Make a class kindness chain: everyone stand in a line and have the first person (can be you) give a quick high five, handshake, or fist bump to each person in the line and return to your original place in the line. The second person turns to go down the line as soon as he has been greeted, then the third person turns, and so on until everyone has greeted everyone in the class and is back in their places.

- Sitting in a circle, ask students to share one of their favorite activities or memories from *Peace of Mind* class this year.
- Have the puppets Paco and say goodbye to the students one final time.

* as described in Week 9, students "pop" to the front of the room, show and describe their work, and then call the next student as they pop to put away their work and return to the circle. This can take quite a bit of time for everyone to do.

Closing: *Goodbye, class! I hope all your senses are filled with peace this week and every week until we see each other again!*

Optional Lesson Extension:

Book – *What Does Peace Feel Like?* By Vladimir Radunsky. Read this book to the class for additional ideas on what peace smells like, tastes like, looks like, and so on.

Week 32
Peace in Me

OBJECTIVES: Evaluate concepts of self-calming learned throughout the year to select those that are most helpful.

PREPARE: Bell or chime; one "Peace In Me" page per student (see Appendix)

> ASCA Standards:

B-SMS 7.Demonstrate effective coping skills when faced with a problem

B-SS 1. Use effective oral and written communication skills and listening skills

Opening: *Hello stupendous students! Did anyone use their Peace skills since I saw you last? If you did, I want to hear about it!*

Call on students to share their experiences.

Mindfulness Practice

Say: *Class, we are at the end of our **Peace of Mind** journey for the year. Let's remember all the ways we practiced mindfulness:*

> **Mindfulness Practice**
> * Belly breathing and other ways to take deep breaths (animal breaths, and so on.)
> * Noticing our feelings and thoughts
> * Practicing heartfulness and feeling thankful for others
> * Using our five senses very deeply to notice more around us
> * Scanning every part of our bodies and relaxing our muscles
> * Using our imaginations to pretend to be in a calming place
> * Using positive self-talk and heartfulness to tell ourselves kind and encouraging words

Say: *Today during the Mindful Moment you will again have the power to choose the activity that feels good to you. When I ring the bell, listen until it stops and then choose to do one or more of the skills we practiced this year. I'm going to be quiet so you can be mindful all on your own. After I ring the bell a second time, we'll raise our hands, open our eyes, and tell what mindfulness activity we chose to use today.*

Invite students to get in their mindful bodies and to take three deep breaths together. Ring the bell once. Close your eyes and place your hands in your lap.

After a sustained period of quiet time, ring the bell again. Raise your hand, open your eyes, and invite children to share which mindfulness activities they chose today.

Say: *I'm so proud of you for being able to choose your own way to practice mindfulness. Since our **Peace of Mind** classes are almost finished, it will be important for you to know how to have a Mindful Moment on your own after school is over for the year.*

 Lesson

Say: *All year long we've learned about different ways to help our bodies feel calm and peaceful. You just practiced some of the ways we do that. Now we're going to draw your favorite ways to get your body calm.*

Facilitate a short discussion about each of the mindfulness skills, modeling them yourself briefly, and/or use the puppets to recall and model skills learned throughout the year.

After discussing the above points, distribute the Peace in Me pages for students to complete. Students should choose one or more of the icons representing a mindfulness skill at the bottom of the page and incorporate them into their picture. Complete the picture by adding personal characteristics to make the body resemble your own.

Depending on how much time you have, choose any or all of the following closing activities:

- Play popcorn* to have students come up and share their Peace in Me picture with the class.

- Pair students with their Kindness Pals to show each other's Peace in Me pictures, and give each other compliments on their books.

- Make a class kindness chain: everyone stand in a line and have the first person (can be you) give a quick high five, handshake, or fist bump to each person in the line and return to your original place in the line. The second person turns to go down the line as soon as he has been greeted, then the third person turns, and so on until everyone has greeted everyone in the class and is back in their places.

- Sitting in a circle, ask students to share one of their favorite activities or memories from *Peace of Mind* class this year.

- Have the puppets say goodbye to the students one final time, if they haven't already done so.

* as described in Week 9, students "pop" to the front of the room, show and describe their work, and then call the next student as they pop to put away their work and return to the circle. This can take quite a bit of time for everyone to do.

Closing: *What an amazing year together it has been, peacemakers. Have a wonderful, peace-filled summer, and remember that you have the power to help create peace in yourself, wherever you are!*

Resources

Reproducible
Materials for Lessons

Reproducible Handouts

Week 2 - Flower picture for belly breathing

Week 6 - Kindness Pal list template

Week 8 - Feelings Thermometer

Week 9 - Thought bubble template

Week 16 – Diagram of the Brain

Week 31 - Peace Booklet

Week 32 - Peace In Me template

Week 2 - Flower Picture for Belly Breathing

Breathe in through nose

Blow out of mouth

Week 6 - Kindness Pals List

for the week of _____

	Student	Student
1.		
2.		
3.		
4.		
5.		
6.		
7.		
8.		
9.		
10.		
11.		
12.		
13.		
14.		
15.		

Week 8 - Feelings Thermometer

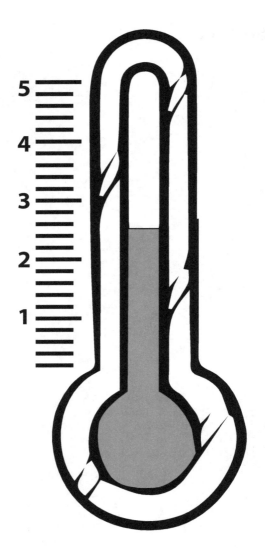

Week 9 - Thought Bubble

Week 16 – Diagram of the Brain

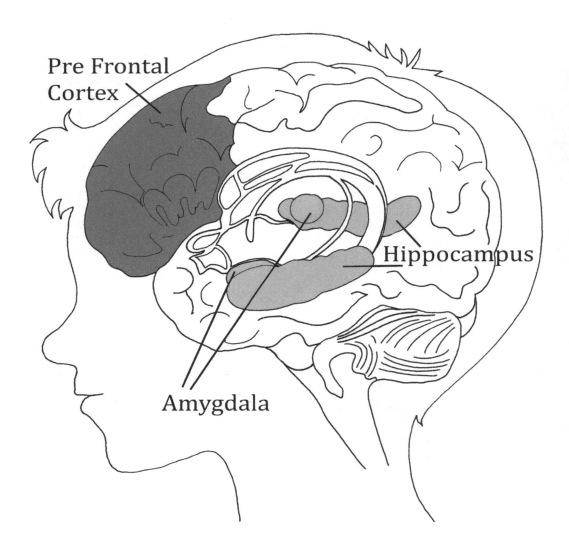

Week 31 - Peace Booklet

Booklets will need to be prepared by an adult ahead of time as follows:

1. Fold paper in half longwise, along the bolded line

2. Fold the *Peace sounds like/tastes* like flap on the line towards the middle box

3. Fold the *front cover/Peace looks* like flap on the line towards the middle box so that it is in front

4. Cut along the dotted line to separate the pages

5. Put one or two staples in the spine to hold booklet together

Peace tastes like:

Peace sounds like:

Peace smells like:

Peace feels like:

What is Peace?

Peace looks like:

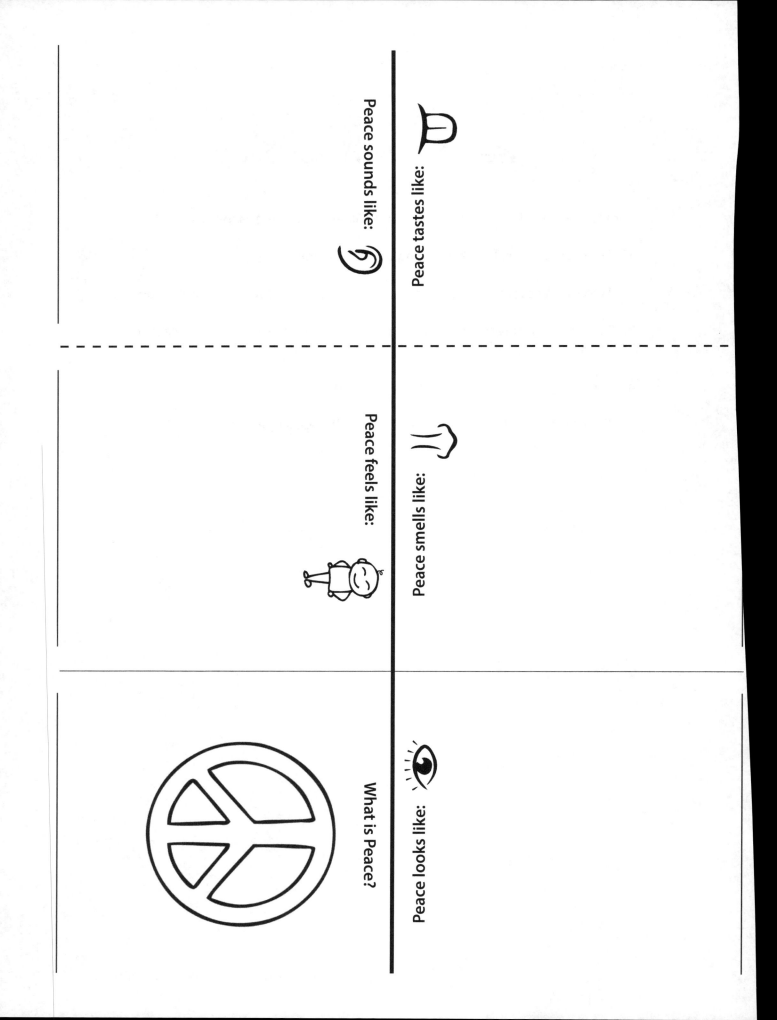

Week 32 - Peace In Me

My Mindful Moment Choices

Flower breathing

Noticing feelings

Noticing thoughts

Gratitude

Heartfulness

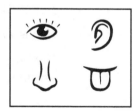

Mindful Senses

Body Scan/Muscle Relaxation

Visualization

Positive Self-talk

|

Books, Videos, and Card Decks Used in Lessons

Books

- *A Children's Book About Teasing* by Joy Berry (in the *Help Me Be Good* series)
- *Everyone Matters* by Pat Thomas
- *Glad Monster, Sad Monster* by Ed Emberly and Anne Miranda
- *Have You Filled A Bucket Today?* by Carol McCloud
- *Howard B. Wigglebottom Learns About Sportsmanship: Winning Isn't Everything* by Howard Binkow
- *I Will Never Not Ever Eat a Tomato* by Lauren Child
- *It's Okay to be Different* by Todd Parr
- *My Many-Colored Days* by Dr. Suess
- *Sally the Sore Loser: A Story About Winning and Losing* by Frank J. Sileo
- *Share and Take Turns* by Cheri J. Meiners
- *Should I Share My Ice Cream?* by Mo Willems
- *Swimmy* by Leo Lionni
- *Take A Deep Breath* by Sue Graves
- *The Berenstain Bears and the Trouble With Friends* by Stan Berenstain
- *The Day No One Played Together: A Story About Compromise* by Donalisa Helsley
- *The Fantastic, Elastic Brain* by JoAnn M. Deak
- *The Peace Book* by Todd Parr
- *The Recess Queen* by Alexis O'Neill and Laura Huliska-Beith
- *The Sneetches* by Dr. Seuss
- *The Thankful Book* by Todd Parr

- *The Zax* in *The Sneetches and Others Stories* by Dr. Seuss
- *Today I Feel Silly* by Jamie Lee Curtis
- *Waiting is Not Easy!* by Mo Willems
- *What Does Peace Feel Like?* by Vladimir Radunsky
- *What is A Thought? (A Thought is A Lot!)* by Amy Kahofer and Jack Pransky
- *When My Worries Get Too Big* by Kari Dunn Buron
- *Whole Body Listening Larry at School* by Elizabeth Sautter and Kristen Wilson

Videos – All available at Youtube.com

- *Belly Breathe* by Sesame Street
- *Cookies of the Caribbean* by Sesame Street
- *Fill Your Bucket* by The Learning Station
- *Sesame Street's "Word of the Day is Conflict"*
- *Star S'Mores* by Sesame Street
- *The Biscotti Kid* by Sesame Street
- *Furry Potter* by Sesame Street

Card Decks

- Peace of Mind's Mindfulness Practice Cards
- *Feelings Flashcards* by Todd Parr
- *Yoga Pretzels: 50 Fun Yoga Activities for Kids and Grownups* Card Deck by Leah Kalish and Tara Gruber

Resources for Teachers and Parents

Videos

Dr. Siegel's Ted Talk video on hand model of the brain http://www.drdansiegel.com/resources/everyday_mindsight_tools/

Sesame Street's Cookie's Crumby Pictures series on self-regulation, including14 videos parodying popular movies

Apps

Smiling Mind: this is a free app from Australia that helps kids practice mindfulness https://smilingmind.com.au

Headspace: this is a mindfulness app that is for adults but could be used by older elementary students as well. It isn't a free app but you can try out ten sessions for free. www.headspace.com

Books with CDs (for kids and adults)

Sitting Still Like a Frog by Eline Snel

A Still Quiet Place by Amy Saltzman

Building Emotional Intelligence by Linda Lantieri

Books for Adults

The Mindful Child by Susan Kaiser Greenland

Mindfulness: an Eight-week Plan for Finding Peace in a Frantic World by Mark Williams and Danny Penman

Wherever you Go There You Are by Jon Kabat Zinn

Ten Percent Happier by Dan Harris

The Way of Mindful Education: Cultivating Well-Being in Teachers and Students by Daniel Rechtschaffen

Bibliography & Credits

Bibliography

Bradshaw, C. P. (2015). Translating research to practice in bullying prevention. *American Psychologist,70*(4), 322-332. doi:10.1037/a0039114 http://psycnet.apa.org/journals/amp/70/4/322/

Buron, K. D., & Curtis, M. (2012). *The Incredible 5-point Scale: The Significantly Improved and Expanded Second Edition: Assisting Students in Understanding Social Interactions and Controlling Their Emotional Responses.* Shawnee Mission, KS: AAPC Inc.

Buron, K. D., & Myles, B. S. (2013). *When My Worries Get Too Big!: A Relaxation Book for Children Who Live With Anxiety.* Shawnee Mission, KS: AAPC Publishing.

Congleton, C., Hözel, B. K., & Lazar, S. W. (2015, January 08). Mindfulness Can Literally Change Your Brain. *Harvard Business Review.* https://hbr.org/2015/01/mindfulness-can-literally-change-your-brain

Edwards, S. P. (2005, May). The Amygdala: The Body's Alarm Circuit. *BrainWork.* An online publication of The Dana Foundation. http://www.dana.org/Publications/Brainwork/Details.aspx?id=43615

Euston, D., Gruber, A., & Mcnaughton, B. (2012). The Role of Medial Prefrontal Cortex in Memory and Decision Making. *Neuron,76*(6), 1057-1070. doi:10.1016/j.neuron.2012.12.002

Gold, A. L., Morey, R. A., & Mccarthy, G. (2015). Amygdala–Prefrontal Cortex Functional Connectivity During Threat-Induced Anxiety and Goal Distraction. *Biological Psychiatry,77*(4), 394-403. doi:10.1016/j.biopsych.2014.03.030

Greater Good Science Center. Expanding the Science and Practice of Gratitude. Retrieved March 23, 2017, from http://greatergood.berkeley.edu/expandinggratitude/

Harrison, H. (2016, March 17). How to Teach Your Kids about the Brain. Mindful. http://www.mindful.org/how-to-teach-your-kids-about-the-brain/

Harvard Health Publications (2011, November). In Praise of Gratitude. http://www.health.harvard.edu/newsletter_article/in-praise-of-gratitude

Kannan, V. (2015, July 15). Understanding and Practicing Heartfulness. http://en.heartfulness.org/blog/2015/07/15/understanding-and-practicing-heartfulness/

Langer, E. (2011) "Mindfulness and Mindlessness" *The Production of Reality: Essays and Readings on Social Interaction*. Thousand Oaks, CA: Pine Forge Press.

Lantieri, L., & Goleman, D. (2014). *Building Emotional Intelligence: Practices to Cultivate Inner Resilience in Children*. Boulder, CO: Sounds True.

Lantieri, L., & Zakrzewski, V. (2015, April 7). How SEL and Mindfulness Can Work Together. http://greatergood.berkeley.edu/article/item/how_social_emotional_learning_and_mindfulness_can_work_together

Madrigal, S., Winner, M. G., & Knopp, K. (2008). *Superflex: A Superhero Social Thinking Curriculum*. San Jose, CA: Think Social.

Metz, S. M., Frank, J. L., Reibel, D., Cantrell, T., Sanders, R., & Broderick, P. C. (2013). The Effectiveness of the Learning to BREATHE Program on Adolescent Emotion Regulation. *Research in Human Development,10*(3), 252-272. doi:10.1080/15427609.2013.818488

Mischel, W. (2015). *The Marshmallow Test: Understanding Self-Control and How to Master It*. London: Corgi Books.

Phelps, J., MD. (2014, December). Memory, Learning, and Emotion: the Hippocampus. Retrieved March 23, 2017, from http://psycheducation.org/brain-tours/memory-learning-and-emotion-the-hippocampus/

Schnabel, J. (2009, December 16). Prefrontal Cortex May Be Key in Controlling Anxiety. Retrieved March 23, 2017, from http://www.dana.org/News/Details.aspx?id=43024. An online publication of The Dana Foundation

Schonert-Reichl, K. A., & Lawlor, M. S. (2010). The Effects of a Mindfulness-Based Education Program on Pre- and Early Adolescents' Well-Being and Social and Emotional Competence. *Mindfulness,1*(3), 137-151. doi:10.1007/s12671-010-0011-8

Stewart, R., MD. (2015, February 24). Amygdala Hijack – Your Brain In Emotion Overload. http://www.engagedactiontraining.com/amygdala-hijack-your-brain-in-emotion-overload/

Svokos, A. (2014, December 01). Watching Cookie Monster Can Improve A Child's Self-Control. http://www.huffingtonpost.com/2014/12/01/cookie-monster-self-control_n_6227008.html

Weare, K. (2013). Developing mindfulness with children and young people: a review of the evidence and policy context. *Journal of Children's Services,8*(2), 141-153. doi:10.1108/jcs-12-2012-0014

Zoogman, S., Goldberg, S. B., Hoyt, W. T., & Miller, L. (2014). Mindfulness Interventions with Youth: A Meta-Analysis. *Mindfulness,6*(2), 290-302. doi:10.1007/s12671-013-0260-4

Zenner, C., Herrnleben-Kurz, S., & Walach, H. (2014). Mindfulness-based interventions in schools: a systematic review and meta-analysis. *Frontiers in Psychology,5*. doi:10.3389/fpsyg.2014.00603

Credits

Week 5 – The Concentration Circle by Sean Layne, Founder of Focus, 5, Inc. www.ArtsIntegrationConsulting.com

Week 16 – **Hand Model of the Brain:** "Everyday Mindsight Tools." Dr. Dan Siegel. March 17, 2011. http://www.drdansiegel.com/resources/everyday_mindsight_tools/

Acknowledgements

This curriculum guide would not be possible without the guidance and support of many wonderful people. First and foremost thanks to Linda Ryden, my fellow teacher, mindfulness mentor, and dear friend for setting the stage for this program at Lafayette Elementary School, and for guiding me down the pathway to Peace. Thanks also to Cheryl Dodwell, our editor, visionary, and brain-in-chief at Peace of Mind. Surely this would not be a movement without your wise counsel!

Thank you to the wonderful administrators at Lafayette, who supported the growth and expansion of Peace of Mind over the years and were willing to "buck the system" and prioritize the emotional well-being of our students over many other potential uses of time during the instructional day. These include Lynn Main, Jackie Snowden, Carrie Broquard, and Stephanie Mayhew. We certainly wouldn't be here without your support, leadership, and out-of-the-box thinking.

Thank you to all the amazing pre-kindergarten and kindergarten teachers and assistants who have welcomed me into your classrooms, sat with me for a Mindful Moment with your class, and continued using mindfulness with your classes after I left. You are amazing educators, each and every one of you! Your love and patience with your students has been an inspiration and example to me, and I've tried to channel your collective demeanor in the scripts and teaching tips detailed here.

Thank you especially to my dear friend and colleague Irene Taguian for your constant enthusiasm for this project, for letting me try out new lessons with your Pre-K class, and for your awesome photography of our work together!

Finally, thank you to my family for your patience and willingness to support me in this multi-year endeavor, for countless hours helping to make puppets, and to my kids especially for your candid feedback on every lesson and activity included this book. I vow to not spend early mornings, late nights, and whole weekends buried in the computer anymore and to be fully present in our family (until the next project presents itself, at least!)

With gratitude,

Jillian

Author Bio

Jillian Diesner directs the Early Childhood implementation of *Peace of Mind* at Lafayette Elementary School and collaborated with Linda Ryden to create the *Peace of Mind* curriculum, Early Childhood edition.

Jillian is a certified School Counselor and formerly certified Special Education teacher who works with students at Lafayette Elementary School, a public school in Washington, DC. She teaches weekly *Peace of Mind* classes to all Pre-Kindergarten and Kindergarten students at Lafayette. She is a Licensed Professional Counselor in the District of Columbia, holds Masters' degrees in Early Childhood Special Education from the George Washington University and in Marriage & Family Counseling from the University of Florida. She has trained in mindfulness through Mindful Schools and with Linda Ryden.

An avid traveler, Jillian currently lives in the Washington, DC area with her husband and two rambunctious boys, who helped inspire her journey into mindfulness ☺

Notes

CPSIA information can be obtained
at www.ICGtesting.com
Printed in the USA
LVHW061124160919
631173LV00013B/229/P